# DIZZY GILLESPIE

D1241996

# DIZZY GILLESPIE
## and the Be-Bop Revolution

Raymond Horricks

*Selected discography*
by Tony Middleton

**Spellmount**
TUNBRIDGE WELLS

Hippocrene Books
NEW YORK

First published in UK in 1984 by
SPELLMOUNT LTD
12 Dene Way, Speldhurst
Tunbridge Wells, Kent TN3 0NX

ISBN 0 946771 10 3

British Library Cataloguing in Publication Data

Horrocks, Raymond
    Dizzy Gillespie.—(The Jazz Masters)
    Gillespie, Dizzy  2. Jazz musician—United States—Biography
    I. Title  II. Series

First published in USA in 1984 by
HIPPOCRENE BOOKS INC
171 Madison Avenue
New York, NY 10016

ISBN 0 88254 908 1

*Series editor:* John Latimer Smith
*Cover design:* Peter Theodosiou

*Cover:* Dizzy Gillespie at the Capital Radio Jazz Festival,
London, 1979.
*Title page:* The High-Priest of Be-bop, Nice 1983.

Printed & bound in Great Britain
by Anchor/Brendon Ltd, Tiptree, Essex

for Justine Gabrielle, again, and for Clara and Britt Woodman
also for Liz and David Driver

# Illustrations

*Cover:* Dizzy Gillespie at the Capital Radio Jazz Festival, London, 1979. (Tim Motion)

*Title page:* The High-Priest of Be-bop, Nice 1983. (Tim Motion)

Diz 'n Bird. (Jan Persson)

With Teddy Mill's band. (Max Jones)

Leading his own 1946 band Howard Johnson, now with The Savoy Sultans, is the saxist on the left. (Max Jones)

A jam session at Eddie Condon's Club. Also involving Jo Jones, Pee Wee Russell, Milt Jackson and Gerry Mulligan. (Max Jones)

With James Moody and Max Roach. (Hans Harzheim)

With Clark Terry and Harry Edison. (Hans Harzheim)

With James Moody at Nice 1983. (Tim Motion)

With Herbie Hancock at Nice 1983 (Tim Motion)

'Those who had the *entrée* entered the private apartments by the mirror-door that gave on to the gallery and was kept shut. It was only opened when one scratched at it and was closed again immediately.'

SAINT-SIMON (at the Versailles of Louis XIV)

'You just don' mess with Diz. I mean, he's a very warm and generous person, and if you're at a jam session and you play in your own style then everything's okay. But he's also very proud of the trumpet-style he largely invented, and if you try to take him on in *that* way, well then, you're going to be cut to ribbons.'

THAD JONES (speaking to the author)

# DIZZY GILLESPIE

DIZZY GILLESPIE has been the most influential jazz trumpet-player since Louis Armstrong. In between these two men the other important trumpeter is Roy 'Little Jazz' Eldridge; and since Dizzy there has been Miles Davis. But Roy acted as a kind of John the Baptist before Dizzy's coming; while Miles' individuality grew as a variation on the Gillespie foundations.

Add to this the fact that the man himself is not just a pioneer of modern jazz but also a virtuoso on his chosen instrument and one has the necessary start to any written profile of him.

The Be-bop Revolution in a sense became inevitable. In a free society each generation rebels or reacts against the values and methods of its preceding, parental generation almost as certainly as day follows night. Only the moment when this occurs is a variable factor. For as Malcolm Cowley states so accurately in his book *A Second Flowering*, 'A generation is no more a matter of dates than it is one of ideology. A new generation does not appear every thirty years . . . it appears when writers of the same age join in a common revolt against the fathers and when, in the process of adopting a new life style, they find their own models and spokesmen.'

In this case he is speaking of course in literary terms, and of that marvellously endowed group of creative spirits, born between 1894 and 1900, who were dubbed – with comic irony – by Gertrude Stein 'The Lost Generation'. Of Scott Fitzgerald, Hemingway, John Dos Passos, e. e. cummings, Thornton Wilder, Faulkner, Djuna Barnes, Tom Wolfe and Hart Crane. But this is still a good way of describing what happened to jazz in the early 1940s. A group of talented younger musicians were restless, frustrated; they wanted a place in the sun and determined to find it by over-throwing the authority of New Orleans jazz, Dixieland and finally too the Swing bands.

In more musical terms, it represented a change from the simpler melodic variations to improvisation based on different, and sometimes difficult harmonic progressions, thus creating a new type of melody. A change in rhythm was involved as well: from the straight, 4/4 beat of the 1930s to a fragmented, even polyrhythmic effect more closely related to the phrasing of one or more brass and reed instruments. The string-bass became the real pivot of the rhythm section now; with the drummer enjoying

11

greater freedom, the acoustic guitar suddenly being plugged into an electrified box called 'an amplifier' and the pianist providing precise chordal support for the frontline soloists. Naturally again, such drastic alterations gave rise to a need for fresh composition. Often, with the arrogance, self-righteousness but also the self-confidence of youth and youthful ideas they would build fascinating, tricky themes over the chord structures of popular, standard songs. Which got them out of having to pay Performing Rights Society fees – and kept everyone except very clever musicians off the bandstand. 'We didn't want those old cats coming up and playing with us. So we made sure they just couldn't cope' (Kenny Clarke). Add Gillespie's own words here: 'There were some who couldn't blow at all but would take six or seven choruses to prove it. So on afternoons before a session Thelonious Monk and I began to work out some complex variations on chords and the like, and we used them at night to scare away the no-talent guys. After a while we got more and more interested in what we were doing as music, and, as we began to explore more and more, so our music evolved.'

'Be-bop' itself is a semi-meaningless word: originally coined to describe the sound of a phrase played by Dizzy. But it has associative convenience when applied to the dawning of the revolutionary movement which we refer to as the first modern jazz of the 1940s. The modernists took their cues from various ideas and/or attitudes of otherwise disparate soloists who belonged to the Swing era: and these have to be considered in a profile of Gillespie. Men like Roy Eldridge and Harry Edison; but above all Lester Young. Other soloists coming out of Swing (the pianist Clyde Hart, for instance) helped with the bridge-building. And then there are the trumpeter's great contemporaries, Charlie Christian and Charlie Parker. Both of these need to be discussed and their relationships with him. The credit for the modernists' own various discoveries is not always easy to apportion. Leonard Feather has endeavoured to isolate individual devices. 'In California in 1940 Oscar Moore, guitarist with the King Cole Trio, ended the group's first Decca record, *Sweet Lorraine*, on a ninth chord with a flatted fifth (an unheard of departure then, an overworked *cliché* today). At Café Society in New York, Kenny Kersey, pianist with the Red Allen Sextet, found his way from a tonic to a dominant chord through an unconventional progression of minor sevenths.' On the other hand, neither Moore nor Kersey showed anything beyond a passing interest in the modern movement.

Essentially of course at this stage, the revolution developed well away from the ears of the public. It grew inside certain men's minds; and within their exchanges of ideas. In retrospect all we can base our judgements on are the leftover manifestations. Which usually means on disc – and those of the very early 'forties be-bop are pitifully few. Or again we can believe the remembrances of those who took part.

One fact is beyond argument though. The first modern jazz increasingly came to revolve about, and became – quite deliberately – the 'exclusive' property of a small group of dissidents who met up for some informal jamming at Minton's Playhouse in New York City. (West 18th Street, next to the rather shabby Cecil Hotel.) 'As for those sitters-in we didn't want, when we started playing these different changes we'd made up, they'd become discouraged after the first chorus and slowly walk away . . .' (Kenny Clarke).

Henry Minton, a former saxophone-player and Harlem's delegate to Local 802, New York's branch of the American Federation of Musicians, had opened this small club for jazz people to meet and relax in – or to play there if they liked. It had a bar, a bandstand, even a small restaurant. 'It wasn't a large place, but it was nice and intimate. The bar was at the front, the cabaret in the back. The bandstand was situated at the rear of the back room, where the wall was covered with paintings depicting weird characters sitting on a brass bed, or jamming, or talking to chicks.

'During the daytime, people played the jukebox and danced. I used to call in often and got many laughs. It's amazing how happy those characters were – living, dancing and drinking. It seemed everybody was talking at the same time; the noise was terrific. Even the kids playing out on the sidewalk danced when they heard the music.' (Mary Lou Williams)

'Things began at Minton's in the terms of modern jazz in the latter part of 1940. Until then the place had been frequented by old men, cronies of Mister Minton.' (Kenny Clarke) The difference came after ex-bandleader Teddy Hill was installed as manager. 'He asked me to bring in a band. Yes, even though he had fired me from his own band several years before because I was beginning to play modern drums! Anyway, when Teddy took over, Minton's changed its music policy. Teddy wanted to do something for the guys who had worked with him. He turned out to be a sort of benefactor since work was very scarce at that time. Teddy never tried to tell men how to play. We played just as we felt.' (Clarke)

So they could concentrate all night if they wanted on their (consciously) difficult new themes: adamant that the 'old guard' would be kept right out of all they were getting together by way of melodic, harmonic and rhythmic development.

In no time the club was a proving ground for the more important modernists. For Charlie Christian, Dizzy Gillespie, Thelonious Monk, Kenny Clarke and soon, inevitably, Charlie Parker. Other early adherents included the pianists Bud Powell and George Wallington, bassist Oscar Pettiford (first disciple of the great, dying Jimmy Blanton), a young, gifted drummer called Max Roach, composer Tadd Dameron and tenor-saxist Allen Eager. 'People dug the music we were playing. They used to come from miles around – from Chicago, from everywhere to hear us play. Most of them were musicians, but there were others who weren't. People would make it *a must*. Earl Hines and the guys with his band would drop by and play with us. Dizzy would be there and Roy Eldridge, Lips Page and Georgie Auld.' (Kenny Clarke)

However, and before going into the importance of Charlies Christian and Parker and Dizzy's other close associates at the time of Minton's, and then moreso into the position of Dizzy himself, it's necessary to insert three thumbnail-sketches of the trumpeter's (and be-bop's) forerunners. Only two of these are fellow trumpet-players; the third man played the tenor-saxophone and I will write of him first.

LESTER YOUNG, 'Pres' to his colleagues (a nickname bestowed on him by Billie Holiday), was born in New Orleans, graduated then to the Kansas City jamming school and began to receive national attention from 1937 when he toured and recorded with Count Basie. He was a true changeling: a great soloist of the

Swing era who expressed his discontent with it in a style which made him the virtual Voltaire of the modern movement. His teachings tremendously influenced the later men; but then he himself took no further part in be-bop (as I suspect Voltaire would have reacted against the eventual violence of France's Revolution). Perhaps Parker and Gillespie progressed just too far for him. Or was it that he felt slightly safer *within* the very musical class he'd originally rebelled against?

'Frankie Trumbauer was my first idol,' Lester later recalled. 'He played C-melody saxophone. I tried to get the sound of a C-melody on tenor. That's why I don't sound like other people. Trumbauer always told a little story. And I liked the way he slurred the notes. He'd play the melody first and then after that, he'd play around the melody.' But, as he admitted: 'Every musician must try to be his own stylist. There's a time when you have to go out and tell *your* story.'

Lester's method of story-telling comprised a soft, flattish-sounding tone and a quietly ingenious, legato way of phrasing, indicating that it was possible to improvise freely, sincerely and imaginatively without the sometimes excessively agitated attack of previous jazz forms. He called for relaxation, and a more reflective approach to improvisation – with the soloist taking a devious rather than an obvious path to the variations he played on a theme. This new path showed up the themes in a different light, most of all harmonically, but it did not cause any loss of swing.

'Lester used more notes and less notes than his predecessors,' Ross Russell has written: 'But abundances were balanced against bareness within the structure of his solos. His musical thought flowed, not within the accepted confines of two or four-bar sections, but more freely. He thought in terms of a new melodic line that submitted only to the harmony of the original as it reworked the melody into something fresh and personal. The chord and bar changes are arranged with such adroitness that the listener is frequently not aware of them until after they have fallen. Lester's way is to phrase ahead – to prepare for and gracefully lead into the next stage several beats before its arrival. To be able to move so freely, in and out of the harmonies with an ear so keen and a step so sure, to always come out on the right note and beat – this is a mark of genius.'

Lester's delivery was airy, but above all *free*. And behind his surface relaxation there lurked a very nimble mind: bent on the less-obvious, but in no way less-creative ideas. He could take and bend a theme, twisting it, squeezing out its ultimate essence, in the end totally transforming it. 'The sound of Lester on those old Basie records – a really beautiful tenor-saxophone, pure sound. How many people he's influenced – how many lives!' (Lee Konitz)

After Lester it became possible for many younger jazzmen to say as with Gauguin: 'You have known for a long time what it is I wish to establish. *The right to dare everything.*'

The two trumpet-playing forebears of Gillespie had an altogether different significance.

LOUIS ARMSTRONG (1900-71), the first great soloist of jazz, had broken up the old 'collective frontline' playing of the initial New Orleans period and single-mindedly turned his instrument into an outlet for individual virtuosity. He had completely dominated the 1920s with a style that was hot, forceful and used technique in a startlingly inventive way. At this time it could be said of him, like Shakespeare's *Julius Caesar*: 'Why, man, he doth bestride the narrow world like a Colossus'. He was also more daring rhythmically than the early New Orleans men, taking liberties with his phrasing and accentuation to reinforce the chain of ideas. Moreover, he evidenced an intense and soaring lyricism; and although in his turn Dizzy Gillespie would reinterpret and restructure jazz phrasing on the trumpet he has never tried to pull away from Armstrong's attacking qualities. The hot tone remains an essential ingredient of his work. Likewise the open and extreme emotion.

ROY ELDRIDGE came along in the 1930s, when suddenly there were a number of fresh trumpet developments. Rex Stewart within the Duke Ellington orchestra began edging towards a more personal style: the growling, half-valve effects and new experiments with mutes which would produce such solos as *Menelik – The Lion of Judah*. Henry 'Red' Allen was playing melodic intervals never before heard in jazz. And there were two exciting young stylists in the Count Basie band: Buck Clayton and Harry 'Sweets' Edison. But Eldridge became the real catalytic cracker for trumpeters of the later 1930s.

In 1927 – aged sixteen – he had disappeared from his home in Pittsburgh to play with a travelling show, The Nighthawk Syncopators. He couldn't read music yet, and the only way to keep the job was by learning note-for-note and then playing on his trumpet Coleman Hawkins' tenor-saxophone solo *Stampede* (recorded with Fletcher Henderson). He then copied more of Hawkins' solos and a couple by Benny Carter. Quite unconsciously, therefore, he had bypassed the influence of Louis Armstrong and unlocked the gates leading to a new method of phrasing. Years later, in New York City, Roy did listen to Louis properly – and says he gained in melodic continuity from the experience. Also a knowledge of how to build climaxes. But by this time his own style was already formed.

The basis of the Eldridge method, which is with Harry Edison's a bridge to Dizzy Gillespie's playing, can be traced back to those very saxophone solos he pirated in his youth. It is a lot faster than Armstrong normally played – including abrupt internal tempo-changes. There are also more notes to each phrase, and he runs over the chords of a piece as easily and flexibly as a sax-player would. Similarities even exist between the contours of the lines he improvises and the melodic variations of Hawkins and Lester Young, his early masters. A style based purely on adaptation therefore? No, not entirely, because Roy then added certain qualities of his own. He is a spontaneous, emotional force when he plays: capable of blistering heat and above all great drive. Moreover, provided the company is good, he quickly becomes excited and will seek to push himself beyond the natural limits. It can result in some startling jazz. He will reach for high notes that Louis never attempted, and usually make them. He is agile, brilliant, unpredictable. There is less sense of form than in Armstrong's (or Gillespie's) best solos, but one hardly notices this as he bursts into flame and the ideas cover you like an eruption of laval sparks. 'Roy's feelings push his valves down, not his fingers.' (Don Ferrara) After this, and then adding what he discovered in the jazz before and at Minton's Playhouse, at last the formation of Dizzy Gillespie's original style had lift-off . . .

Meanwhile, returning to Minton's again, things were

beginning to happen there at a very rapid rate indeed – and largely triggered, before the full flowering of Charlie Parker and Dizzy Gillespie, by the guitarist Charlie Christian.

Thelonious Monk on piano was now formulating a lot of the jagged new harmonies, while Kenny Clarke's drumming introduced the distinctive cross-rhythms, extra beats and punctuation. But Christian was really the Che Guevara of the modern movement: the intrepid revolutionary who died young. Dizzy, although an equally important revolutionary, reminds one more of Fidel Castro: a pragmatist, firmly built and who has lasted. Charlie Parker, the one undeniable genius of the Be-bop Revolution, figures somewhere between the two of them.

CHARLIE CHRISTIAN was a revolutionary in almost everything he did. Already before him Django Reinhardt had introduced a style of single-note picking on the jazz guitar. But this came out in delicately poetic fragments of melody, stemming from his own ethnic roots. I doubt whether Christian, born in 1919 in Dallas and raised in Oklahoma City, knew very much about musical poetry – or about European folk forms. What he did know about was his own folk music: the Blues. And he had the nerve to turn *this* form inside out. Furthermore, because of tours with various local combos, he'd encountered the jamming in Kansas City and understood what was being preached musically there. Especially the sermons wafting from Lester Young's tenor-saxophone. It wasn't long before Charlie (as with Roy Eldridge) could improvise lines like a saxophone's on his own instrument, long and apparently effortless single-note lines based on the chords instead of being a series of purely melodic variations, and squeezing further harmonic juices out of his blues background. In order to edge closer still to the tonal sound of Lester's tenor, he began experimenting with an amplified guitar – which in turn led to his lifting the guitar out of the jazz rhythm section and phrasing it alongside the horns or as part of the ensemble.

Charlie had reached more or less this stage when John Hammond visited Oklahoma City and heard him there. A telegram and some later persuasion resulted in an audition with Benny Goodman. 'They played *Rose Room* for forty-eight minutes! John (Hammond) had been in on most of Goodman's triumphs . . . but he never saw anyone knocked out as Benny was that night. Apparently, Charlie just kept feeding riffs and rhythm and changes for chorus after chorus. That was Benny's first flight on an electronically amplified cloud.' (Bill Simon)

Christian stayed with the Goodman band until early in 1941 when a recurrence of tuberculosis made it impossible to carry on. He died the following year, aged not quite twenty-three. Many of his performances with Goodman are based on his own thematic figures and indicated a further stage of revolutionary development. For Charlie was by now imposing more drastic changes on the Blues. Changes to chords, which he saw his way clear to opening up even more so than Lester Young had done, running eighth-note phrases, and including what were considered strange intervals like a ninth, a flatted ninth or – his own favourite – the diminished seventh. Changes also to the traditional melodic lines, now pulled apart and rebuilt on riff figures almost identical to those later composed by Parker and Gillespie for their unison-ensemble small groups. And finally rhythmic changes. For although Christian could be a formidable swinger in even 4/4 time (Basie's beat), this was not enough for him. He began to accent and then to augment the classic drive of the 'thirties; using off-beats in the most surprising places, frequently subdividing the beat from 4 to 3 and so on. All of which he carried forward with him to the after-hours sessions at Minton's.

There Charlie was able to improvise at length, and to meet and work with other dedicated modernists. He became part of the unofficial 'house' band along with Kenny Clarke and Monk. It was made easier by the Goodman band being resident in New York City at this time. The guitarist just grabbed a taxi from one job to the other. Often Dizzy Gillespie would drop by and then the jazz really took off, for Charlie could exchange ideas for as long as the trumpeter wanted to play. Other musicians came and went, some good, some mediocre (like Joy Guy), but until he was too sick to play Charlie wailed at the club every night. He had a second amplifier built for Minton's; and he never rested between sets, which didn't help his physical condition.

He became a vital influence on those musicians who had the chance to play with him; and the majority testify that he was both helpful and challenging. If he were alive today his stature would be enormous. Instead of which, in 1940/41 he fired the opening salvos signalling that the modern movement must now come out into the open and become an established force. Then he was gone. . . . Finally, one other – obvious – musician who has to be discussed in relation to Dizzy Gillepie.

CHARLIE 'YARDBIRD' PARKER: Following the death of Charlie Christian these two men would completely dominate be-bop/modern jazz for the next decade and a half. I once wrote that Charlie Parker was a jazz explorer with a fine sense of harmony as his compass. And 'Bird' himself recalled 'One night before Monroe's I was jamming in a chilli house on Seventh Avenue between 139th and 140th. It was December, 1939. Now I'd been getting bored with the stereotype changes that were being used all the time, and I kept thinking *there's bound to be something else.* I could hear it sometimes but I couldn't play it. Well, that night, I was working over *Cherokee,* and, as I did, I found that by using the higher intervals of a chord as a melody line and backing them with appropriately related changes, I could play the thing I'd been hearing. I came alive!'

In fact, he came to superimpose chord changes faster than any other saxophone player before him. So fast that one night at Minton's, when Bird was using a borrowed tenor, the formidable Ben Webster went up and snatched the instrument out of his hands. 'That horn ain't s'pposed to sound that fast,' he announced angrily. 'But that night Ben walked all over town telling everyone, *Man, I heard a guy – I swear he's going to make everybody crazy on tenor.* The fact is, Bird never felt tenor, never liked it. But he was playing like mad on the damn thing!' (Billy Eckstine) However, dexterity was only one of Parker's attributes: and subject to his inventiveness.

He was born in Kansas City in 1920, and at fifteen was already on the road playing with Jay McShann's band. Unfortunately, this also exposed him to the seamier side of modern American life before his early innocence was completely shed; which resulted in his becoming addicted to the ghastly toll of heroin. He played with several other groups – but in the main these were rootless years for him, while personal unreliability tended to lose him jobs almost as soon as he'd landed them. But then, from early 1941 Charlie was in New York all the time and, when he could borrow a saxophone (alto or tenor), appearing at Minton's most nights to play and swap ideas with Dizzy, Monk, Kenny Clarke *et al.* It became clear to each of them that this was the one player modern jazz could not do without.

From early in 1943 he was with Earl Hines' band and lasted a year. Often, as Billy Eckstine remembers, the rest of the men would be covering up for Charlie's falling asleep on the bandstand; or under it! Dark glasses helped. Then in 1944 he toured with Eckstine's own big band; his final job as a sideman. Afterwards, the sudden acceptance of be-bop by the East Coast public enabled him, either to play in a quintet with Dizzy, or lead one of his own along New York's 52nd Street.

With a unison-ensemble frontline of trumpet and alto-saxophone this would remain his chosen musical formula until near the end of his life. It certainly became the framework for most of his greatest records and in turn had a tremendous influence on the younger jazzmen who grew to idolise him. Once Dizzy had his mind set on the idea of a bigger band, Parker turned to using Miles Davis or Kenny Dorham on trumpet. His favourite pianists – like Dizzy's at this period – were the fastidious, but still superbly swinging Al Haig, then later on Duke Jordan. They also used Bud Powell on occasions, but Bud was too like Bird's own explosive personality for the two to be completely comfortable together. On drums there was usually Max Roach, the first disciple of Kenny Clarke and the most brilliant one.

Mention of the altoist's personality is a reminder of course that his creativity was very dependent on current mental and physical conditions. For Charlie's output frequently fell into the terrible grip of his addiction. Once, on the West Coast, he had to drink a quart of whisky to make the recording session, collapsed in the middle of it and was then packed off to the State Hospital. Hence his later composition, *Relaxin' at Camarillo.* At other times, when comparatively free from the problem, his music reached a level of inspiration unsurpassed in modern jazz. He played with a dazzling co-ordination of mind and fingers. His imagination was so fertile that we are only just beginning to recover from the shock

21

waves.

For he was a complete voice; with no apparent influence after Basie's Buster Smith on him except the Blues and the sessions he had been a part of with Dizzy Gillespie at Minton's. Also, like Christian and Dizzy, Charlie detested boundaries – and he would use his great technique to cross them. His dramatic changes of rhythm, the swift surging back and forth into double-time, the insertion of brittle, staccato runs between the more flowing, legato phrases: these were in effect his wirecutters. His technique also gave him power to break down practically all the chordal barriers of traditional jazz. He subscribed to the theory of eventual atonality in music; and, although he never lived to apply this to jazz, nevertheless it summed up his approach: namely that a soloist's invention cannot be expected to obey academic rule-books. Technique without a broad avenue of expressiveness he regarded as useless. And he moved from a melodic to a harmonic source when he found this helped his own melodic inventiveness. 'Modern jazz,' he once said, '. . . is an attempt to play cleanly and to search for the pretty notes.' In his own case, Charlie might have added that beauty emerged with his selection of what were (often) the more difficult notes and intervals between notes; and swing in spite of the broken be-bop rhythms, for with him swing belonged inherently.

Adjacent to this there was the distinctive feature of his tone. An intensely personal, and very much a vocalised tone, well away from the earlier, silkier ones of Benny Carter and Johnny Hodges. It made for a clear and piercing sound; yet rich and bitter like the taste of an olive. Also it suggested all the immense emotional tension of character in his playing.

Again, I find a sense of urgency and an obvious soul in what he did: such as only one musician from each generation of jazz may have in ideally balanced quantities. Though he had lots of new things to say, nevertheless Bird was but an extension to the main traditions of the music. When he recorded his famous slow blues, *Parker's Mood*, in 1948 he created for the listener a most moving experience. It's as if one is listening to a younger brother of Louis Armstrong or Sidney Bechet. And because of this it's much easier to understand the newer things he had to say.

In 1949, in Paris, Charlie unfolded what appeared to be the

realities of the new music before me within the space of a single concert. *Very forcefully and very clearly.* 'Suddenly to stumble upon an artist of this calibre or an instance of his work,' I wrote later, 'is its own Book of Revelations. A sketch by Daumier. A couplet by Pope. What vistas an accidental discovery can open up for the previously uninitiated!' I was suspicious enough of modern jazz at this time. I was young then, and the critical thunderheads were still gathered over it in both the United States and Europe. Yet, from the moment Parker walked on-stage in his crumpled chalk-stripe suit and began to play, I knew − instantaneously − that the new jazz would outlive its critics. Canadian writer Daniel Halperin recalls being stunned by Bird's playing in Paris. 'Afterwards,' he told me, 'I just wandered up to an all-night *café* by the Place Clichy, I ordered a drink and then another, and I was still sitting there when the baker's boy came in at dawn with fresh *croissants*, still thinking about Bird!'

Since then, I've always thought of Parker, not merely as a genius-player, but in addition as an essential, musical and continuing conscience for jazz: governing the modern movement's otherwise free, and at times irresponsible will. Ross Russell calls his definitive biography of C. P. 'Bird Lives!' And certainly everyone who matters in the music today keeps on referring back to and relating with him . . .

Charlie Parker died on March 12, 1955 at the age of thirty-four. He died in the apartment of the Baroness Koenigswarter while watching the Dorsey Brothers on television, and the autopsy revealed that death was due to cirrhosis and the longterm effects of heroin.

However just one week before this he had bumped into Dizzy Gillespie outside Basin Street East. Desperate, down-and-out, he had pleaded with Diz, 'Let's get together again. I want to play with you again before it's too late.'

'Dizzy can't get over Bird saying that to him,' Lorraine Gillespie recalls. 'His eyes get full of water even now when he thinks about it. He was downstairs a week after that meeting at Basin Street when I heard all this crying, and I found out someone had called and told him Charlie was dead. I didn't say anything; what could you say? I just let him sit there and cry it out.'

Words which are as good an introduction as any to the fascinating, twinned trines of Dizzy Gillespie's character. He *is* a warm, generous man, devoted to his friends and, with his great natural humour, determined to entertain, to satisfy his host of admirers.

As just one instance of his many personal kindnesses, I will insert here a story told me by Keith Goldson, the blind guitarist and composer. Originally from Jamaica, but for many years a resident in Britain, when he speaks of Gillespie there is still a lot of emotion in his voice. 'It was by the River Thames when I first met him. At Meadhurst where British Petroleum has a sportsground. I'd been parakit(e)ing, not the easiest thing for a blind man to do, but it was for charity. Anyway, he (Dizzy) turned up with his friends Jimmy and Janet Wright, apparently wearing an enormous Stetson – which of course I couldn't see. But he then went out of his way to praise what I'd done. I mean this man is a giant, a legend in his own lifetime, *praising me!* Not only that, he then inisisted that my wife and I (she's blind too) go up to Ronnie Scott's as his personal guests – and when we got there he'd arranged everything, the table, drinks, everything. And afterwards, after he'd played he came down, put his arm round my shoulder and said that any themes I write I should mail off to him direct. Since then I've dedicated one to him, a piece called *Dizzy Flight*. But then, I believe, that's him. He's just as impressive a man as he is a trumpeter.'

At the same time though, no one should ever try to outwit him. He's very businesslike, a brilliant organiser and probably the most calculating of the first modern jazzmen. 'Dizzy like a fox' Teddy Hill once called him. In 1956, and as a world-famous figure, over the weeks of the State Department band tour of the Middle and Far East he was paid a higher salary than that of the-then U.S. President, Dwight D. Eisenhower. Later, when the band went to Ecuador and he learned of the rarefied air up in the Andes around the capital Quito, that night he let Joe Gordon take all the trumpet solos. Joe, young and eager to show off his abilities, agreed without giving it a thought – and the concert nearly killed him . . .

Nevertheless, Dizzy has lasted. He's never been into dope, he seeks out and eats healthy food and, even today, while still capable of turning out marvellous solos, he never loses sight of the fact that it's important for a man to pace himself. After blowing a series of amazing, lip-shattering, octave-up choruses for example, he'll play the next number on conga drums or maybe piano. At other times he travels his young (and brilliant) *protége*, Jon Faddis, to share the trumpet chores. He remains aware, absorbent *and thinking;* but always extrovert, exuberant and – to an appreciative audience – wildly exciting. Behind the sometimes scat-singing and general clowning of the man one must not lose earshot of the great gifts he undoubtedly possesses. He became the leading soloist of the true modern jazz after Charlie Parker; was the first musician to collect the new ideas and players into group formats, both small and large; and has continued to be the finest, most unorthodox trumpet-player of his age. Perhaps it's not so surprising that his favourite relaxation is playing chess – and to a fairly high standard . . .

His real name is John Birks Gillespie; hence the title of one of his best-known compositions, *Birks' Works. Dizzy* was appended much later, the result of his jokey and deliberately eccentric behaviour with certain big bands. He was born in Cheraw, South Carolina on October 21, 1917, the ninth and last child of Mrs Lottie Gillespie (only six of whom survived). The family background was modest, but – unlike Bird's – there was much love around, which is probably significant. 'My father treated my mother real good,' Dizzy later told Richard Boyer of *The New Yorker.* 'He got her real expensive stuff. I was scared of him though. When he talked, he roared. He was a real man. He didn't have a voice like this,' and the trumpeter ended on a falsetto note. 'I got a beating every Sunday morning. At school I was smart, but I didn't study much. I'd fight every day. I was *all*-ways bad, you know!' So again: love and firm discipline.

On the other hand it was due to his father that he first became aware of real music. Although a bricklayer by profession, Gillespie Senior ran a local band on the side and their different instruments were usually stored in the house. The young Dizzy liked to fool around with them. *When his old man was out of course!*

Later, in 1927 when his father died he won a scholarship to the Laurinburg Institute in North Carolina, a Negro industrial school where he could also study music theory and harmony. At fourteen he started playing trombone, didn't like it and borrowed a friend's trumpet. Soon he acquired one of his own, but did not study it formally and only learned to sight-read with it a few years after this. In 1935 the family moved to Philadelphia and as a result Dizzy missed graduation. He would be awarded his diploma two years later.

In Philly, now aged eighteen, he landed a job with the Frank Fairfax band – where he teamed up with Charlie Shavers, a cousin, and another trumpeter Carl Warwick, who would one day be in Dizzy's own bands. His own playing by this time was very much under the influence of Roy Eldridge – but he could gauge that something quite different was likely to happen, and once it did he wanted to be present at the creation.

In 1937 he actually took Eldridge's place in the Teddy Hill band. They were getting ready to tour Europe. However, due to his unorthodox approach to the new scores (he'd try out the interludes and climaxes first), as well as his comedy imitations of the other band members and his strange sartorial habits (he began to appear in a beret and sported a long cigarette-holder), several sidemen threatened to quit if he wasn't fired before the tour got under way. In the end Teddy Hill managed to calm things down; but Dizzy was relegated to the third trumpet chair. The only solos he played in Europe were at off-duty jam sessions at 'The Nest' club in London.

Back in New York afterwards, he had a six months' waiting period before he could obtain a Local 802 card. Then he rejoined the Hill band: at forty-five dollars a week; and also met his future wife, the dancer Lorraine Willis.

Most of the Hill sidemen still regarded the things Dizzy was working hard to unscramble through his horn as insane. Kenny Clarke didn't though. When he joined Teddy Hill on drums in 1939 Dizzy was the only other musician in the band who really interested him. Clarke was deep within his own experiments at this stage; breaking up the straight 4/4 time with accents and superimposed rhythms. He started reading trumpet-parts and could follow their phrasing. Dizzy began reading drum-parts, and phrasing with them. In Cab Calloway's band over the next two years he would often jam with bassist Milt Hinton and found he could phrase with that instrument too. Moreover, while with Calloway he at last got on record as a soloist: *Pickin' The Cabbage* (his own theme and arrangement), *Hard Times* and a groovy *Bye-Bye Blues.*

From 1940 when Kenny Clarke took the remnants of Teddy Hill's band into Minton's the new modernism began to crystalize. Every time Cab Calloway played New York Dizzy would be there. He'd already absorbed Kenny Clarke's rhythmic teachings. Now, playing alongside Clarke, he was exposed to pianist Clyde Hart and the exhaustive compositional probings of Thelonious Monk; plus as well everything Charlie Christian was doing. It was some months later that Charlie Parker started falling in. By which time Dizzy was already three-quarters *en route* to being his own man – and obviously a kindred spirit.

'Dizzy . . . was becoming very advanced . . . and was the first one I heard play *How High The Moon* in any other tempo than what had been the usual slow tempo up to then.' (Kenny Clarke) To which Gillespie adds: 'I was with Cab by this time – when I first started hanging out with Thelonious (Monk) and I don't think Cab could figure out at all what I was trying to blow out of my horn on his stand.'

Milt Hinton is more specific though. 'When Dizzy came into the Calloway band in the early 'forties the first impression he made was that he was very progressive – even more than Chu Berry. Chu and Dizzy didn't hit it off too well. They'd played together before with Teddy Hill. Chu was the star with Calloway and Dizzy wasn't . . . but Chu's style was based on riff patterns and speed. Dizzy's music was much more exciting. It wasn't perfected yet. There were things he attempted to do that he couldn't. I admired him for what he tried though. Like he'd try a long-range progression with a high-note at the end and he missed it. Cab would get angry, and some of the guys in the band would say, *Nice try, kid, try it again.* But most of them didn't think he'd amount to anything.

'I was a kind of laboratory for Dizzy in the Calloway band. It was easy to get a bass aside so I'd walk him on bass while he'd try different chords and progressions.'

Another Calloway sideman, guitarist Danny Barker confirms that between shows Dizzy and Hinton would go off together and that 'what they were doing called for a lot of mental concentration on harmonies. Dizzy was very energetic and a fine, likeable chap. He had none of the jealousy or the envious traits that a lot of the big stars acquired.

'Cab had some wonderful arrangements in his book. Sometimes after the show . . . he'd play for dancing. Dizzy would take his solos and Hinton would follow his patterns. Often, what Dizzy played would be contrary to the arrangement. But Milt would look at me and I'd bend the chord to fit in. It sounded interesting and beautiful to me, but it angered Cab . . . who would point at Diz and say, *I don't want you playing that Chinese music in my band.*

'But Diz continued to work on those beautiful patterns, and I believe that was the real start of the new sounds. Next thing I heard there was a character in town called Bird and another one called the Mad Monk and they all worked together at Minton's.'

Anyway, over that next year or so of Minton's a synthesis seems to have occurred which gave the trumpeter his dynamic method of playing. But it would not have been possible without Dizzy's developing a superb technique to accommodate it. He extended the normal range of the jazz trumpet to go even higher than Roy Eldridge had done; and he could play phrases of some complexity up there instead of merely hitting single notes. Again he learned to play very fast; but with flexibility. Fast enough to breast the tape with Charlie Parker; sufficiently flexible to play long, intricate solos over the most difficult of Monk's chords. Only his tone remained close to Eldridge now: a hot, stinging, open-faced sound.

To return to the synthesis though. This included a little of what everyone who mattered at Minton's was doing plus some fresh ideas of his own. From working with Kenny Clarke (and Milt Hinton) there came about almost an interdependence of melody and rhythm. One element tended to define the other: so that a Gillespie solo, his interspersing of rapid runs with even, on-the-beat phrases and so on fitted with the accents, rhythmic breaks and syncopation of the accompaniment. Possibly from Clyde Hart (1910–45) came the smoother, more flowing and pianistic aspects of be-bop improvisation – which in turn led to more new compositions (often using the harmonies of earlier songs like *How High The Moon* and *I Got Rhythm*). After playing with Monk, Dizzy could make good use of unlikely harmonic progressions, of surprising intervals, and the calculated use of dischords. While to Charlie Christian the debts were sometimes obvious, sometimes less so. An obvious one was the insertion of fast, eighth-note phrases; a more indirect one would be the superimposing of a new chord on the basic progression, suggesting different keys but remaining harmonious. Finally, from Charlie Parker he took certain cues on how to make a fresh, rich and exciting melodic language out of all these devices. But the ingenious insertion of grace notes and passing chords into the contours of his improvisation was entirely his own. Likewise the blowing of riff-figures based on the be-bop harmonies. And his interest in cross-breeding alien rhythms with jazz, i.e. *Night In Tunisia,* plus the later Afro-Cuban experiments . . .

The end with Cab Calloway occurred in September, 1941 with what was in reality the last wild fracas of Gillespie's youth. He would never lose his sense of humour (happily), but after this incident he ceased to be irresponsible in front of an audience, and in fact proceeded to become one of the most mature and reliable leaders in jazz. As the story goes, on the night in question he was wrongly accused of throwing spitballs in the middle of a show in Hartford, Connecticut. The real culprit was fellow-trumpeter Jonah Jones. The leader/showman – who regarded himself as the only allowed purveyor of comedy on-stage – was still annoyed with Dizzy for trying to outscore him on previous occasions and after the show this led to an altercation in the wings. Or rather in the seat of Calloway's trousers. 'Cab made a pass at Diz,' is how Milt Hinton remembers it, 'and was nicked in the scuffle before they were separated. He hadn't realised he'd been cut until he was back in the dressing-room and saw all the blood.'

'Cab Calloway still has a sore end,' *Down Beat* magazine gloated afterwards. 'Cabell took ten stitches from a doctor.' What they should have added is that at this period and even today many musicians carry knives and some also have guns: purely for self-protection. I can remember on one occasion being amazed to witness Roy Eldrige opening his trumpet case – and there lying beside his horn was what looked like a West Indian machete or cutlass. Now Roy happens to be one of the most lovable people you could ever hope to meet – and he noticed my surprise. 'Baby,' he said, 'if you go down South, or even just here in New York after an extra-late gig, when all those junkies and muggers are around, then you gotta have something.'

Following the departure from Calloway, Diz worked with Ella Fitzgerald and wrote pieces for Woody Herman and Jimmy Dorsey. Then he played – in rapid succession – with Benny Carter, Charlie Barnet, Les Hite and Lucky Millinder. But be-bop was the new force to be reckoned with and he determined to stay involved. It finally began to take off late 1942–43 when he was with the Earl Hines big band and then properly in 1944 with the short-lived, immensely talented Billy Eckstine band.

The Hines band had incorporated Charlie Parker as well; if he turned up and was capable of playing. But the Eckstine band was virtually a travelling kindergarten for modern jazz. For although Gillespie, Bird and others who would make modernism a public sensation congregated in Hines' band during 1943 they were seldom able to express their ideas on the bandstand. Earl was musically sympathetic, and he admired their talent and dedication. 'They used to carry exercise-books with them and would go through the books between shows when we played the theatres.' But his own commercial policy still adhered to big band Swing. So the revolutionaries continued to keep the outward manifestation of their experiments for after-hours at Minton's. Until, that is, singer Billy Eckstine (whom Hines dubbed 'the black Sinatra') decided to feature them in his own band's playing. For in the next 'key' period – from June 1944 until 1947, when pure economics forced Billy to go solo – almost every important younger modernist passed through its ranks, prior to their exploding into a wide variety of small groups in and around New York City.

Nowadays of course Billy Eckstine is one of the most respected popular singers in the world. In 1944 though he was only just beginning to make a name for himself nationally. So when he decided to lead a band the experienced Budd Johnson (also ex-Hines) did most of the organising and wrote part of the book; the remaining scores were written by Dizzy, Tadd Dameron and trombonist Jerry Valentine. 'About nine other guys came over from the Hines band.' (Eckstine) Plus Sarah Vaughan, who was developing into the most instrumental-sounding of all jazz-singers. Meanwhile too the leader had located Charlie Parker again, this time in Chicago, and hired him. He also 'stole' a young drummer, Art Blakey, from Fletcher Henderson's orchestra.

Given the benefit of hindsight, as Eckstine sees it: 'Progressive jazz or bop was a new version of old things, a theory of chords and so on. I said Bird was responsible for the actual playing of it and Dizzy put it down. And that's a point a whole lot of people miss up on. They say *Bird was it!* or *Diz was it!* – but there were two distinct things.

'The whole school would listen to what Bird would play; he was so spontaneous that things which ran out of his mind – which he didn't think were anything – were classics. But Diz would sit there, and whatever he played, he knew just what he was doing. It was a pattern, a thing that had been studied. He's got that mind of his that people often don't stop to figure on. He's one of the smartest guys around. Musically, he knows what he's doing backwards and forwards. So what he hears – that you think maybe is going through – goes in and stays. Later, he'll go home and figure out just what it is. So the arranging, the chord progressions and so on, Dizzy is responsible for. You have to say that.'

Over the next three years the band's changing personnel reads rather like a Burke's Peerage of modernism: Dizzy Gillespie, Fats Navarro, Miles Davis, Kenny Dorham and 'Little Benny' Harris, trumpets; Bennie Green, Jerry Valentine and Howard Scott, trombones; Charlie Parker and Junior Williams, alto-saxophones; Budd Johnson, Dexter Gordon, Gene Ammons and Lucky Thompson, tenor-saxophones; Leo Parker (no relation to Bird) on baritone-saxophone; John Malachi, piano; Tommy Potter, bass, and Art Blakey the drummer. Eckstine himself played occasional valve-trombone solos, but essentially concentrated on giving the band popularity through his singing. Unfortunately, despite all his efforts, the musicians were always atrociously recorded. Bad balances between the sections and a general lack of definition reduced to a mere shaving what observers agree the band sounded like 'live'. Reissues on LP are of interest historically and for excitement, but still decidedly lo-fi.

However: as Leonard Feather has written, 'It was an era of discovery. Dizzy never tired of playing; one night in Chicago he persuaded Oscar Pettiford to trudge through ten long blocks in a snowstorm, carrying his bass, to join him in a hotel room for an all-night jam session. Often in New York, up at Dewey Square, or at Dizzy's apartment nearby, there would be Bud Powell and Benny Harris and Freddie Webster, to whom playing and talking and thinking meant more than eating and drinking. When Dizzy wasn't at home practising or writing arrangements, he'd be Downtown taking private lessons with a trumpet teacher.' Incidentally, when he plays his cheeks go out and his neck inflates like a balloon: all of which is highly unorthodox for trumpet-players. No matter. He was assured that this would do him no physical damage – and that's the way he's played ever since.

He stayed less than a year with Eckstine. After which he began to use his additional talents as an organiser to create the various small groups which would propagate the new jazz; both in New York and then across the continent. Sometimes Parker became a member, and each man must have contributed to the idea of a trumpet and saxophone playing intricate be-bop themes together over a (generally) guitar-less rhythm section. Parker is often credited with developing this unison-ensemble quintet formula, because already Gillespie had his mind firmly set on translating Charlie's and his own ideas to *the* eventual big band. Even so, Dizzy was still the first to collect any modernists for club work outside Minton's and in this, the *Annus Mirabilis* of be-bop (1945) everyone who mattered played in his groups along 52nd Street. 'When Diz and Bird hit the Street regularly . . . nobody could get near their way of playing music. Finally though they made records, and then guys would imitate it and go on from there.' (Tony Scott)

He was subjected to some of the most savage attacks ever perpetrated against a jazz musician by the *soi-disant* critics of the day. Who afterwards, having got it all wrong, would then pretend they'd never said the things they did. But the public, as usual ahead of the critics, began to get it right. In 1944 the more discerning *Esquire* had voted Dizzy the greatest 'new star' on trumpet; after which the old guard jazz magazines began to fall down as swiftly as the walls of Jericho.

Some of the anti-Gillespie faction, again to quote Leonard Feather, make interesting reading. Especially since several now make money either writing about or recording modern jazz. Nesuhi Ertegun (the current President of WEA): 'The American public is misled . . . the outlook for jazz is gloomy. Only by returning to New Orleans jazz can it become a living art form again.' Then Ernest Bornemann (in *The Melody Maker*) 'The boppers are sophisticated, urbanised Negroes . . . the result is disastrous . . . they have sold their birthright for a poisoned mess of pottage.' John Hammond, once a jazz fan, but since then the record producer of Bob Dylan: 'Bop is a collection of nauseating *clichés*, repeated *ad infinitum*.' And George Frazier: 'This is incredible stuff for a grown man to produce.' Impresario Norman Granz said 'Jazz in New York stinks! Even the drummers sound like Dizzy Gillespie. There isn't one trumpet player in any of the clubs except Hot Lips Page. Charlie Parker's combo is rigid and repetitive.' In fact this last statement is the most hilarious of all, because eventually Granz swallowed his considerable pride (and his words) and asked both Dizzy and Bird to record for his labels.

Meanwhile though Dizzy remained undeterred. The new jazz had made it and be-bop (his revolution as much as anyone's) had established its own kingdom in the face of the old monarchies.

In 1946 he recorded a classic date for RCA Victor with Don Byas (tenor-saxophone), Milt Jackson (vibraharp), Al Haig (piano), Bill De Arango (electric guitar), Ray Brown (bass) and J. C. Heard (drums). The titles were: *52nd Street Theme, Night In Tunisia, Anthropology* and *Ol' Man Re-bop*. Apart from signposting that a fresh approach to jazz composition had occurred (the first three themes are still played in almost every country of the world every night), they also – via his truly remarkable trumpet solos – declaimed that the clock could not now be turned back. His high-octave chorus during *Anthropology* alone has joined Louis Armstrong's *West End Blues* and Eldridge's *Wabash Stomp* in the jazz Hall of Fame. And so it went on. His only failure had been the year before, when at Billy Berg's in Hollywood the audiences, somewhat behind New York in jazz awareness, preferred the guitar-comedy act of Slim Gaillard to Dizzy's music. This was the tour when Bird got so sick and why, back in The Apple, Don Byas took his place the the RCA

*Anthropology* session. Otherwise it was public acclaim all the way; and even if the critical argument still raged Dizzy's name had also reached Europe. Everyone who hadn't yet heard him play was madly curious to do so.

All revolutions though, as with dictatorships, have their in-built risk factor. Once they succeed then the ideals, ideas and interests of the leaders tend to diversify, and even pull in different directions. The most famous revolution of all, the French, is a case in point. It began as a middle-class revolt against the king and the tax-free, but all-powerful aristocracy. Manipulation of the workers and peasantry gave the revolutionaries a cutting edge; but then it was lawyers and other interested parties who came to dominate the Paris Convention. Whereupon the divisions immediately revealed themselves: resulting in a second struggle for power which came to a head (or rather several heads) when Robespierre succeeded in sending his fellow-Jacobins Georges-Jacques Danton and Camille Desmoulins to the guillotine. Subsequent to Robespierre's own downfall, the inefficiency and corruption of the Directory under Paul Barras brought about the political vacuum through which Napoleon passed so easily on his way to the top.

Of course I'm not suggesting the Be-bop Revolution resulted in any personal violence. But once established its leaders still went their separate ways. Charlie Parker wanted to lead his own quintet; which when he ran out of trumpet partners became a quartet, and by the end of his life he was touring with a somewhat gluey string section. The pianists Bud Powell and Al Haig also wanted to lead their own trios. Thelonious Monk ploughed on with his own lonely furrow as a composer. Milt Jackson proceeded to co-found the Modern Jazz Quartet with John Lewis, Art Blakey to form The Jazz Messengers. Dizzy made no secret of the fact that his personal ambition was a big band. And from 1946 to 1950 this is precisely what he led.

In fact he first organised such a band in 1945, called the 'Hep-Sations' of that year – but it foundered when the bookings took it south of the Mason-Dixon line and suddenly 'colour' came back into the picture. Al Haig, being a white pianist in an otherwise black band, refused to go into the Deep South; and there were other defections along the way. The lesson digested, Dizzy then

34

reorganised another band but with what were considered improved prospects – and suddenly in 1946 hit the jackpot! The band's best year of all was 1948. For following this there was a diluted quality of personnel; and by the closing stages, in a mistaken effort to hold audiences, Dizzy's natural flair for showmanship had degenerated into mere Mickey Mouse music.

At the outset he had the services of Gil Fuller, a brilliant arranger whose scores had made such an impressive contribution to the Eckstine band. Gil's prophetic *Things To Come* captured the unabridged excitement and shouting force of the band's sections in the most remarkable way. Others who wrote for it included Tadd Dameron (*Our Delight, Good Bait, Soulphony*) and John Lewis, whose concert work *Toccata For Trumpet and Orchestra* Dizzy premiered at Carnegie Hall in the fall of 1957. At the same time the leader was quick to exploit the phrases of be-bop in a new verbalised form of 'scat' singing, and he now demonstrated a growing interest in the fusion of bop themes with Afro-Cuban rhythms, which in turn led to the savage and intense conga drummer, Chano Pozo joining, to Gil Fuller writing his *Manteca* and eventually to the commissioning of George Russell's *Cubana Be – Cubana Bop* suite.

At its uncompromising best no contemporary big band could equal this one of Dizzy's for excitement and innovation. Crudities abounded: sometimes due to insufficient rehearsal time, more often because of the problems in harnessing the devices of be-bop (essentially a small-group music) to the larger sections of instruments. There was also a noticeable lack of texture (even in the quieter scores of John Lewis). It was brass versus saxophones again, the classic teaching of Fletcher Henderson brought up to date with the new harmonies. Unison riffs (a hallmark of the Swing era) were maintained, although their phrasing became much more intricate. Otherwise there was a 100% endeavour to uphold the Be-bop Revolution and eventually extend it. Lines, figures, chord progressions and rhythmic patterns within the scores strictly adhered to the basic tenets of Minton's. So did the various solos, and the spontaneous combustion of a wildly enthusiastic ensemble. In other words, it was still a recognisable child of what had taken place when Christian and Diz and Parker had joined together for the first time.

In 1948 the band toured Europe. A lengthy tour, from Sweden all the way down to the South of France. New scores included Gil Fuller's *One Bass Hit, Ool-Ya-Koo,* the impressive *Swedish Suite* and his slow solo feature for Dizzy, *I Waited For You;* plus Dizzy's own *Emanon (No Name),* Tadd Dameron's *Stay On It* and John Lewis's *Two Bass Hit* and *Minor Walk.* Lewis had also just completed his *Period Suite* and a fine arrangement of Monk's *'Round About Midnight.* In Stockholm the concerts were marred by a promoter who embezzled the band's share of the takings. But in Paris, under the auspices of Charles Delaunay, Dizzy triumphed.

I have an LP of one of the Paris concerts during which he perfects his interpretation of George Gershwin's song *I Can't Get Started* from 'The Ziegfield Follies Of 1936'. No other jazz trumpeter had tackled this number since the earlier 'hit' record by the late Bunny Berigan; but Dizzy not only took it on, he has now made it virtually his exclusive property.

And upon returning to the States he then triumphed again on the West Coast where previously he'd failed so miserably. Promoter Gene Norman recorded the proceedings on July 26 at the Civic Auditorium, Pasadena. After twenty seconds of the first number on the LP (*Emanon*), one hears a gasp of incredulity and admiration from the audience, followed by a burst of unfeigned applause. Such was the band's great impact. Christmas Night, 1948 at Carnegie Hall witnessed a kind of musical summit. From then on the funny hats took over . . .

After the desperate corn associated with his band in 1950 failed to stave off the ignominy of its break-up Dizzy returned to playing with small groups. Conditions in the U.S. were very much against the big bands by this time – with even Count Basie in trouble and forced to reduce to a septet for a year. Dizzy retained Bill Graham (alto- and baritone-saxes) and his friend Milt Jackson recommended the up-and-coming Wade Legge on piano.

The trumpeter also began to work and record for Norman Granz. And when Graham left the group he chose Sonny Stitt, formerly a tenor-saxophone man, as his regular recording partner on alto. They are particularly good together on 'The Modern Jazz Sextet' (Verve), an LP which at the same time features John Lewis on piano and introduces Dizzy's composition *Tour De Force.*

Diz 'n Bird.

A jam session at Eddie Condon's Club. Also involvin

s, Pee Wee Russell, Milt Jackson and Gerry Mulligan.

With James Moody and Max Roach.

Leading his own 1946 band. Howard Johnson, now with The Savoy Sultans, is the saxist on the left.

With James Moody at Nice 1983.

With Clark Terry and Harry Edison.

*But in 1956 he did lead a big band again*, albeit briefly, and the result of an unusual, unexpected request. He was asked by the American State Department to take a band on 'goodwill' tours of the Middle East, Pakistan (including its then province of East Pakistan, now Bangladesh); and afterwards to South America. This was the first time any United States government had officially recognised the existence of jazz, let alone decided to promote it as a cultural export! But the tours proved enormously successful: for Dizzy personally, for the band and for the U.S. image in the world. 'This music has made our job so much easier,' one ambassador commented.

'Actually Diz was always with cobras or camels or something for publicity purposes, but really I think he enjoyed every minute of it.' (Quincy Jones) Or smoking an enormous Meerschaum pipe and in Athens wearing full Greek national costume! On-stage he appeared the perfect leader: witty, effusive and giving the other musicians lots of encouragement. 'As well as playing a storm on trumpet' (Jones) As regards the goodwill part of his mission, this can best be illustrated by two brief anecdotes. In Karachi, Dizzy was found with a local snake-charmer in his hotel-room. To the embarrassed management he simply replied: 'The man's a musician, isn't he?' Then in Ankara, Turkey he refused to play at a diplomatic garden party until the street urchins crowding outside the walls were let in. 'I came here to play for *all* the people!'

And he was continually pointing to the band – eleven black and four white musicians – adding, *Now watch them work together.* As an aristocratic dowager in Zagreb remarked: 'One concrete example is worth a million words.' Meanwhile the sidemen fraternised with everybody. 'In Dacca,' Marshall Stearns reported, 'where there are few radios and fewer jukeboxes, the audience was puzzled and polite – at first. To them, these were truly new sounds. Then, as they felt the contagious enthusiasm of the band, and, especially, watched the Chaplinesque pantomime of conductor Gillespie, they caught on with a roar, clapped on the right beat, and disported themselves like a mob of rock-and-roll addicts at the Brooklyn Paramount. In Athens, on the other hand, they were neither polite nor puzzled – they took off their clothes and threw them at the ceiling.' GREEK STUDENTS LAY DOWN

45

ROCKS AND ROLL WITH GILLESPIE was one newspaper headline.

Stearns concludes: 'The simple fact is that these audiences – even before they heard it – wanted to love jazz. They associate this music with the relaxed and generous side of American life, and the informal vitality of the performances clinched their convictions. *Let the goodwill roll!* announced Gillespie, and in Communist Yugoslavia the band made a solid point without trying. *You're all so unorganised* stated one party official. *Until you begin to play!*

The main task of assembling and rehearsing this, the third Gillespie big band fell to trumpeter/composer/arranger Quincy Jones, Dizzy being off in Europe on an already-contracted-for 'Jazz At The Philharmonic' tour. 'I was kept as busy as a one-armed paperhanger with lice!' he wrote to me later. However, and in spite of a tough itinerary, the men pressed into service formed a very high-morale crew; and the book they sailed on was an outstanding one, with pronounced emphasis on groove, a wailing attack and an up-dating of the earlier Gillespie band's style of phrasing. Arrangements were by trombonist Melba Liston, who in her *haute-couture* evening gowns was the band's prepared answer to Women's Lib and the veil; Ernie Wilkins and Benny Golson; and of course by Quincy Jones himself.

The latter had developed into one of the finest young talents around by this date. He has since (like Lalo Schifrin) branched out into films and TV writing. But his scores for Dizzy, later on Count Basie and then his own 'This Is How I Feel About Jazz' and 'Birth Of A Band' LPs have found a lasting place in jazz history, while his jazz-rock synthesis 'Smackwater Jack' became a milestone of the 1970s. The acknowledged early influences on him – before listening carefully to Dizzy and Bird and then playing alongside Clifford Brown in the Lionel Hampton band – were Baptist and Sanctified church music, Clark Terry, who taught him to play trumpet, and finally the blind blues singer Ray Charles.

'Ray was seventeen when I was fifteen,' he recalls. 'In Seattle he had a trio called the Maxim Trio. It was a gas! Very modern. Played all the hip things then. Also Ray used to write for a vocal group I was with. One of my very first arrangements was the result of Ray showing me how to voice brass instruments, using

Billy Eckstine's *Blowin' The Blues Away* as an example. And at every jam session in Seattle there was Ray's influence, as strong as a radioactive wave – it always came into them. He played alto, clarinet, piano, organ and he sang the end. To me his blues singing has always told the truth. In fact, my idea of a perfect marriage in jazz would be his feeling with a very full technique to project and develop it.' (Jones, in a further letter to the author)

Which in turn is a reminder that Charles is also a favourite of Dizzy's. 'Do you know what I did today?' he told a friend in the 1960s. 'I went and bought a record. Must be the first time in forty years that I went out *and bought* a record! It's a new thing by Ray Charles. Boy, that cat can *sing!* He gets a real Sanctified church sound, you know? Damn! He's fast becoming my favourite singer!'

Back from the enthusiastic East, there was a hectic (ninety minutes) recording session for Verve. The tour personnel comprised Dizzy, Joe Gordon, Carl Warwick, Quincy Jones and Ermet Perry (trumpets), Melba Liston, Frank Rehak and Rod Levitt (trombones), Phil Woods, Jimmy Powell, Billy Mitchell, Ernie Wilkins and Marty Flax (saxophones), Walter Davis (piano), Nelson Boyd (bass) and Charlie Persip on drums. They recorded Dizzy's *Tour De Force, Night In Tunisia* and *Birks' Works*, plus his perennial flagwaver *The Champ*, this last arranged by Quincy Jones. Jones also supplied an original, *Jessica's Day* and re-scored *I Can't Get Started* for Dizzy; Melba Liston had arranged *Stella By Starlight*, Debussy's *My Reverie* and *Annie's Dance*, based on Grieg's *Anitra's Dance:* Ernie Wilkins' scores included the originals *Dizzy's Business* and *Groovin' For Nat* as well as the arrangement of Horace Silver's *Doodlin';* A. K. Salim wrote and arranged *Dizzy's Blues.* I don't know who arranged Jerome Kern's *Yesterdays*, but it sounds like Melba Liston again; while the final number, Chano Pozo's *Tin Tin Deo* is obviously a 'head' arrangement.

All five trumpeters played the special 45-degree angle instruments: which apparently first came into being by accident at a birthday party for Lorraine Gillespie in January, 1954 at Snookie's Bar along 44th Street. Dizzy had left his horn on the bandstand. A dancer fell over it, so bending the bell part that it was left pointing upwards. After his initial anger had subsided,

Dizzy blew a few notes through it and to his amazement found the sound reached his ears better with the bell tilted up. The next day – always the eager businessman – he rushed around to a trumpet manufacturer he knew to ask if he could patent and produce this new phenomenon. Only, to his *chagrin*, to be told that a similarly-shaped instrument had been brought out 150 years earlier! 'He'd even got himself an order book!' (Lorraine Gillespie) However, because he felt it disseminated the sound in a better way Diz decided to stick with it.

With its recording session out of the way the band then took off for South America and concerts in Ecuador, Argentina, Uruguay and Brazil. Dizzy was so thrilled with everything about this band that he determined to keep it going. They proved a big success at the third Newport Jazz Festival and were still recording for Verve as late as March, 1957. There were some fine new players in it by this time: the 18-year-old trumpeter Lee Morgan, for instance; Al Gray on trombone, Benny Golson on tenor; plus the great Wynton Kelly on piano, a groove-master for all seasons. But the plain truth is that without the State Department's subsidies there were not enough bookings to finance everybody's enthusiasm. When the English drummer Ronnie Verrell visited the United States with Ted Heath's band and bumped into the Gillespie band's drummer Charlie Persip, he discovered the latter had put a stick through the head of his side-drum and couldn't afford a replacement until the band next got paid. Often the men were down to wages of thirty dollars a week. Diz did his best to retain a sense of humour. During a sparsely-attended set at Birdland he still went out and gave them an introductory routine: 'Ladies and gentlemen. I'm sorry we're a little late getting started this evening, but we just came from a very, very important benefit. The Ku Klux Klan was giving a party . . . for the Jewish Welfare Society. It was held at the Harlem YMCA – so you can see we were lucky to be here at all this evening!' Those present chuckled. Even so, on New Year's Eve, 1958 the band played *Auld Lang Syne.*

Still, the man himself is a natural survivor. And he has remained a magnificent soloist. Since 1958 he has toured with (and recorded with) some of the finest small groups in the history of jazz. He has continued to appear in front of big bands, but these have been one-offs, put together for special occasions, such as the festival orchestra at Monterey in 1965 conducted by Gil Fuller. A version of *The Shadow Of Your Smile* by this group, with Dizzy as featured soloist, won a NARAS award nomination in March '66. Also, there was the 1968 'Reunion' band with which Dizzy toured Europe on his way to the Berlin Jazz Festival; and again in 1975 another band the tenorman Billy Mitchell helped put together for several engagements at Buddy Rich's club and which then supported 'A Tribute To Dizzy Gillespie' evening at the Avery Fisher Hall. On this last occasion the trumpeter distinguished himself with an absolutely brilliant performance in the midst of such gifted soloists as Stan Getz, James Moody, John Lewis and Max Roach.

By and large though he has opted for the quintet or quartet formula, travelling his artistry all over the world and gaining immensely in stature with both fans and the jazz Establishment.

One of the earliest and best of his quintets – dating from 1960 – featured Leo Wright on saxes and flute (later replaced by James Moody) and the Argentine-born pianist and composer Lalo Schifrin, who later scored the music for Steve McQueen's 'Bullitt' and is now one of the most respected musicians in the film industry. For Diz, Schifrin wrote *Gillespiana, Tunisian Fantasy* (an extended composition based on Gillespie's own *Night In Tunisia*) and finally *The Lost Continent*, which was first presented at the Monterey Festival in 1962 backed with a large orchestra conducted by Benny Carter.

Dizzy too was busy himself as a composer again. He penned the catchy and intriguing *Con Alma*, a feature at nearly every Gillespie concert since then; *Brother King*, a tribute to the late Martin Luther King; and *Olinga*, dedicated to a Bahai brother, a member of Dizzy's personal religion. Meanwhile he continued to play his classic be-bop themes, *Salt Peanuts, Groovin' High, Blue 'N Boogie, Woody'n You, Shaw Nuff* and *Anthropology:* still favourites with audiences after four decades. Also, there were extra-musical activities. Such as appearing in films: in the 1960s 'The Hole' and in the 1970s Maureen Stapleton's 'Voyage To Next'. Plus his tongue-in-cheek independent candidacy for President of the United States, an event sparked off when a thousand people petitioned the California State Secretary to put his name on the ballot-papers . . .

When James Moody left his group in the late '60s Dizzy replaced him with a guitarist, George Davis. In 1971 the guitarist was Al Gafa and the hard-driving Mickey Roker came in on drums. Roker remained with Diz throughout the '70s and when they appeared in London in 1978 the leader had another heavily-gifted young guitarist in Rodney Jones. Jon Faddis also began to make his guest appearances with the group from the late '70s. An unabashed admirer of Gillespie, he plays in the same style and already, for one so young, possesses an enviable range and technique. At the 1977 Montreux Festival, by some bizarre (management) misrouting the group's rhythm section – Rodney Jones, bassist Ben Brown and Mickey Roker – ended up in Holland. So the two trumpets were backed by Milt Jackson on vibes, Monty Alexander (piano), Ray Brown (bass) and Jimmie Smith (drums). The resulting performances (now available on LP) are among the best trumpet duets ever heard in jazz: exciting without being competitive, alternately heated or soft, but above all never ceasing to be creative in their improvised passages.

With his groups Dizzy has now toured many times in Europe and Asia. He has played in Israel, Tunis, Tokyo and even the Virgin Islands. He is a regular at all the major festivals and never fails to be one of the most-applauded instrumentalists. In 1971-72 he persuaded several of his earlier be-bop companions to drop what they were doing and go on a world tour with him. Even though they were now leaders of their own groups. The outcome was 'The Giants Of Jazz' unit featuring Dizzy with Sonny Stitt, Kai Winding, Thelonious Monk, Al McKibbon and Art Blakey. It gained a brilliant reception everywhere they played. Atlantic Records then issued a 2-LP set based on the concerts in England and Japan, during which the musicians create timeless and (as if by nature) dazzling jazz together. Timeless because of the validity of their musical ideas; dazzling because of their individual and collective greatness as instrumentalists. Dizzy's unaccompanied cadenza playing which opens *Tin Tin Deo* and later his muted work on the same track amount to some of his finest playing on record, *ever.* Likewise Blakey's storming drumming on *Night In Tunisia* and Sonny Stitt's beautiful ballad treatment of *Everything Happens To Me.*

In 1975 he did a similar job of persuasion, but this time towards the studios. 'The Bop Session' (on Sonet), an outstanding LP by any standards, brings together other 'old comrades', Stitt (again) on alto and tenor, pianists John Lewis and Hank Jones, Percy Heath on bass and Max Roach, drums. The be-bop themes they improvise on are all familiar (*Blue 'N Boogie, Confirmation, Groovin' High* and Tadd Dameron's *Lady Bird.*) But there is nothing tired or dated about the way these modern masters play.

In addition Dizzy took part in the Newport-New York Festival's *Tribute to Louis Armstrong*. Despite Armstrong's earlier disparaging remarks about be-bop, by the time of his death he and Diz had become firm friends. The latter has also appeared on many TV shows and is often valued as much for his conversational abilities as for his trumpet-playing. 'People have learned to expect the unexpected of him,' is how Feather-and-Gitler's *The Encyclopedia Of Jazz* puts it. 'As when he stepped out on the stage in the middle of a film and duetted with his screen image at NJF-NY in '75.' I would add to this his surprising and most moving playing in church at the end of Charlie Shavers' funeral service. 'It was totally unexpected,' Phil Payne of *Time-Life* wrote to me. 'Most of us didn't even know Diz had slipped in until he began to blow, very soft and gently from the back. Some of the most beautiful trumpet-playing I've ever heard.'

And of course there have been dozens more recordings, many of the most recent ones for Norman Granz's Pablo label. I particularly like his duets with Oscar Peterson on the 'Jousts' LP (also on Pablo). *Stella By Starlight* and *There Is No Greater Love* here are among the most satisfying of his ballad performances, if one can call them truly ballads, for there are many, very subtle shifts of tempo. Other, earlier recordings are always being re-released, including, naturally, the famous Massey Hall, Canada, concert with Bird, Bud Powell and Charlie Mingus.

One record I would draw the reader's attention to though is the 'Perceptions' LP of 1961. Partly because I don't believe it has ever received the kind of attention it rightly deserves. Also because it stands somewhat apart from the main Gillespie canon. It isn't strictly speaking a jazz work at all but a six-part suite in which there are references to jazz; specially written by trombonist

J.J. Johnson to present Dizzy's trumpet at its most expressive and widespread. As such he is displayed in a way that is often formal, involving every aspect of trumpet-playing, and yet at the same time extremely rich and powerful. Gunther Schuller conducted the 21-piece orchestra, including six other trumpets as well as two harps.

'At the outset,' Johnson says, 'I began to think of what role to cast Dizzy in, and I kept thinking about his playing with big bands. He's a very exciting player. He plays very high and very fast, and can do this just about the best. But I wanted to cast him in a different role because few people realise that Dizzy is also a very sensitive musician with great lyrical gifts. A lot of pieces really don't show off his great capacity for lyricism and melodic playing. I wanted to show more of this sensitive, lyrical side.' Well, this is precisely what he has achieved in the composing. Dizzy's range and technique are phenomenal. Likewise his expressiveness. His jazz abilities notwithstanding, he would be at once the pride and joy of any symphony orchestra he cared to join.

Honours continue to shower down on him like confetti. Apart from the numerous *Metronome* and *Down Beat* awards over the years, including the *DB* Critics' poll from 1971 to 1975, he has an honorary doctorate from Rutgers University, the Handel Medallion from New York City, and a 'Musician Of The Year' award from the Institute of High Fidelity, presented to him by Miles Davis in San Francisco. In the same city he was named 'External Consultant in Ethnomusicology' by the SF School Board, and as such asked to conduct a series of workshops and seminars for young musicians around the area. He has been honoured too in Cheraw, the town of his birth.

None of which has gone to his head. He is still warm and generous, particularly with his time. I can attest to the fact that with ordinary mortals like you and me he is very approachable and easy to talk to. Moreover, although now comfortably off, his life style displays no ostentation, no particular extravagances. He puts this down to his joining the Bahai faith – which includes modesty and the achievement of true simplicity in its teaching that one day all mankind will be united in peace. '*Baha 'u 'llah* is the head of my religious faith,' he explains. 'He said music is a form of worship. I believe it, because in music you must rid yourself of the hangups of racialism and things like that . . .'

He (Dizzy, that is) also said back in 1960, 'What I want to do now is extend what I've done. When an architect builds a building, you know, and decides he wants to put on some new wings, it's still the same building. He keeps on until it's finished, and when he dies somebody else can carry on with it.'

However: it is with the history, the sweep and above all the sheer grandeur of his trumpet-playing that this short, concentrated book has been largely concerned. Qualities which in turn have caused Dizzy to loom large indeed in the history of jazz itself. And I recently came upon some words by an English trumpeter, Ian Carr, which I think are especially appropriate here, reinforcing what I have tried to say earlier about his musical make-up and style.

'He (Dizzy) has a very extensive knowledge of theory and at the same time his instrumental execution matches his thought in its power and speed. He has lightning reflexes and a superb ear . . . and he is concerned at all times with swing. Even when he's taking the most daring liberties with the pulse or beat, his phrases never fail to swing. The whole essence of a Gillespie solo is its cliff-hanging drama. The phrases are perpetually varied. Fast demisemiquaver runs are followed by pauses, by huge interval leaps, by long, immensely high notes, by slurs and smears and bluesy phrases. He is always taking you by surprise, always shocking you with a new thought.'

To conclude though I want to go back to the point Thad Jones made at the very beginning. About the fact that 'you don't mess with Diz'. Because it touches upon the one other point I want to make. And I can best illustrate this by recalling my observations at the 1982 Nice Jazz Festival; or, to be more specific, at the final jam sessions. It was growing dark and on a very hot night. Normally, up on the hill at Cimiez there are light breezes. But this particular night was so hot even the wind had fled. Things were happening on all three stages but the main proceedings took place on what is called 'the arena stage', framed by the Roman arches, old, half-broken walls and sentinel-like *Cupressus* trees.

Promoter George Wein had assembled what can only be described as 'a very mixed bag of players'; which he kept adding to from the other stages. Trumpeter Benny Bailey was there, saxist Red Holloway and of course Dizzy, looking as cool as it was possible to be in a loose *kaftan* and holding the famous 45-degree angle horn. Also Lionel Hampton's vibes had been set up in a prominent position at the front of the stage. I seem to remember the pianist was Jay McShann, with behind him a huge placard advertising a forthcoming production of Verdi's 'Aida'. And the drummer was Gus Johnson. Or was it Oliver Jackson? Difficult to be sure because that part of the stage was in darkness. Anyway, what I can first of all report is that before the arrival of Hampton Dizzy played an extremely exciting duet with Benny Bailey, full of intricate runs and long chase choruses. Then Hamp did arrive and we were set for an extended version of *Flyin' Home.*

Now it's a well-known fact that when Hamp plays at a jam session he just goes on and on, wailing through chorus after chorus, hammering at the notes and gradually building up towards a climax of absolute frenzy and perspiration. This night being no exception. Despite the heat. Except that then, having finally finished his 34 (or maybe it was 40) choruses . . . (the temperature was clearly taking its toll!), he just carried on into the reprise of the theme *and suddenly it was all over.* No chance for the others to get a look in! Poor James Moody, hurriedly dispatched by Wein from the 'dance' stage to join in, was left standing holding his silver-plated flute at the outer perimeter. He hadn't played a single note.

Dizzy was the only one who hadn't been caught napping. He evidently knew Hamp of old – and so 'the fox' came back into play. After the opening theme, like quicksilver he launched into his own solo before the vibes could get started. This over and done with, he was then free to move on in leisurely fashion to the olive garden and join in the other jamming going on down there.

Call it intuition if you like. Call it instinct. But nevertheless it worked wonderfully well for him. I prefer to call it the real Dizzy Gillespie. Who is always aware, always alert, *and always in command of the situation.*

With Teddy Hill's band.

# Postscript

At this point in the book I want to thank my discographer, Tony Middleton for the painstaking nature and high quality of his work. As the reader will become aware, in view of Gillespie's prolific (and continuing) career in the studios, at concerts subsequently issued on disc and with various isolated airshots, unraveling all of this cannot have been an easy task. Although Tony did produce a complete discography for me, space only allowed a selected version to appear in this book.

In addition I too have had a problem with the book. You just can't write a simple straightforward biography of Diz. He has to be viewed from many angles, and some of them as different and unusual as the intervals he plays through his trumpet, or indeed the 45-degree angle of the instrument itself. Most important of all though is the place he occupies in jazz history and its rapid evolution. He has to be seen in his relationships with other musicians, both those who led towards him and those he worked with to forge the iron will of his revolution.

As a trumpet-player he was always destined to be superb. One wonders why he has never recorded Aaron Copland's *Quiet City;* surely as likely a vehicle for him as the *Concierto De Aranjuez* was for Miles Davis. But his position in jazz is greater than his superlative technique. It's what he *did* with the trumpet that has preserved him for all musical time.

*R.H. – Mount Felix, 1983*

# DIZZY GILLESPIE

## A SELECTIVE DISCOGRAPHY

I have based my selections on records generally available at the time of going to press and further listening suggestions follow the main discography. The following abbreviations have been used: (arr) arrangement; (as) alto sax; (b) bass; (bars) baritone sax; (cl) clarinet; (cond) conductor; (d) drums; (fl) flute; (frh) french horn; (g) guitar; (p) piano; (sop) soprano sax; (tb) trombone; (tp) trumpet; (ts) tenor sax); (vbs) vibraphone; (vcl) vocal; all other instruments given in full. Locations: LA (Los Angeles); NYC (New York City). Only records issued in (Eu) Europe and (Am) United States of America are noted. If a record is only currently available in (J) Japan, this too is included.

TONY MIDDLETON *London, February 1984*

# DIZZY GILLESPIE

## A SELECTIVE DISCOGRAPHY

### DIZZY GILLESPIE AND HIS ORCHESTRA

Dizzy Gillespie (tp); Don Byas (ts); Milt Jackson (vbs); Al Haig (p); Bill DeArango (g); Ray Brown (b); J. C. Heard (d). *NYC. February 22, 1946.*

| | | |
|---|---|---|
| D6VB 1682 – 1 | 52nd STREET THEME – 1 | RCA (Eu) PM42408 |
| D6VB 1682 – 2 | 52nd STREET THEME – 2 | RCA (Eu) PM42408 |
| D6VB 1683 – 1 | A NIGHT IN TUNISIA | RCA (Eu) PM42408 |
| D6VB 1684 – 1 | OL' MAN REBOP – 1 | RCA (Eu) PM42408 |
| D6VB 1685 – 1 | ANTHROPOLOGY | RCA (Eu) PM42408 |
| D6VB 1685 – 2 | ANTHROPOLOGY | RCA (Eu) PM42408 |

### DIZZY GILLESPIE with Johnny Richards Orchestra

8 violins; 3 cellos; 2 bassists; frh; harp; violas; woodwinds; Dizzy Gillespie (tp); Al Haig (p); Ray Brown (b); Roy Haynes (d); Johnny Richards (arr, cond). *LA. "Spring" 1946.*

| | |
|---|---|
| WHO | Phoenix (Am) LP4 |
| THE WAY YOU LOOK TONIGHT | Phoenix (Am) LP4 |
| WHY DO I LOVE YOU | Phoenix (Am) LP4 |
| ALL THE THINGS YOU ARE | Phoenix (Am) LP4 |

### DIZZY GILLESPIE SEXTET

Dizzy Gillespie (tp); Sonny Stitt (as); Milt Jackson (vbs); Al Haig (p); Ray Brown (b); Kenny Clarke (d); Alice Roberts (vcl); Gil Fuller (arr). *NYC. May 15, 1946.*

| | | |
|---|---|---|
| 5497 | ONE BASS HIT No. 1 | Phoenix (Am) LP2 |
| | | Prestige (Eu) PR24030 |

# DIZZY GILLESPIE

## A SELECTIVE DISCOGRAPHY

| 5498 | OOP BOP SH'BAM vcl ensemble | Phoenix (Am) LP2 |
| | | Prestige (Eu) PR24030 |
| 5499 | A HANDFULLA GIMME vcl AR | Phoenix (Am) LP2 |
| | | Prestige (Eu) PR24030 |
| 5500 | THAT'S EARLS BROTHER | Phoenix (Am) LP2 |
| | | Prestige (Eu) PR24030 |

### DIZZY GILLESPIE AND HIS ORCHESTRA

Dizzy Gillespie, Dave Burns, Raymond Orr, Talib Daawood, John Lynch (tp);
Alton Moore, Leon Comegeys, Charles Greenlea (tb); John Brown, Howard
Johnson (as); Ray Abrams, Warren Lucky (ts); Pee Wee Moore (bars); Milt
Jackson (p); Ray Brown (b); Kenny Clarke (d); Alice Roberts (vcl). *NYC. June 10,
1946.*

| 5550 | OUR DELIGHT | Bulldog (Eu) BDL 2006 |
| | | Prestige (Eu) PR24030 |
| 5551 | GOOD BLUES vcl AR | Bulldog (Eu) BDL2006 |
| | | Prestige (Eu) PR24030 |

Same as June 10, 1946 except Gordon Thomas (tb) replaces Charles Greenlea.
Add John Lewis (p); Milt Jackson (vbs). *NYC. July 9, 1946.*

| 5609 | ONE BASS HIT No. 2 | Prestige (Eu) PR24030 |
| 5610 | RAY'S IDEA | Prestige (Eu) PR24030 |
| 5611 | THINGS TO COME | Prestige (Eu) PR24030 |
| 5612 | HE BEEPED WHEN HE SHOULD HAVE BOPPED | |
| | vcl AR | Prestige (Eu) PR24030 |

# DIZZY GILLESPIE
## A SELECTIVE DISCOGRAPHY

### DIZZY GILLESPIE AND HIS ORCHESTRA

Dizzy Gillespie, Dave Burns, Elmon Wright, Matthew McKay, John Lynch (tp); Alton Moore, Taswell Baird, Gordon Thomas (tb); John Brown, Scoops Carey (as); James Moody, Bill Frazier (ts); Pee Wee Moore (bars); Milt Jackson (vbs); John Lewis (p); Ray Brown (b); Joe Harris (d); Kenny Hagood (vcl). *NYC. November 12, 1946.*

| 5788 | I WAITED FOR YOU | Prestige (Eu) PR24030 |
| 5789 | EMANON | Prestige (Eu) PR24030 |

Same as November 12, 1946 except Raymond Orr (tp), Bill Shepherd (tb), Howard Johnson (as), Joe Gayles (ts), Cecil Payne (bars) replace John Lynch, Gordon Thomas, Scoops Carey, Bill Frazier and Pee Wee Moore. Add (vcl) to Dizzy Gillespie credits and omit Alton Moore (tb). *NYC. July-August, 1947.*

| THEME (I waited for you) | Phontastic (Eu) NOST7629 |
| GROOVIN' HIGH | Phontastic (Eu) NOST7629 |
| OPP-POP-A-DA vcl DG, KH | Phontastic (Eu) NOST7629 |
| COOL BREEZE | Phontastic (Eu) NOST7629 |
| STAY ON IT | Phontastic (Eu) NOST7629 |
| LADY BIRD | Phontastic (Eu) NOST7629 |
| THEME (I waited for you) | Phontastic (Eu) NOST7629 |
| WOODY 'N' YOU | Phontastic (Eu) NOST7629 |
| TWO BASS HIT | Phontastic (Eu) NOST7629 |
| OOP-BOP-SH'BAM | Phontastic (Eu) NOST7629 |
| HOT HOUSE | Phontastic (Eu) NOST7629 |
| RAY'S IDEA | Phontastic (Eu) NOST7629 |
| PAN-DAMGRONIA | Phontastic (Eu) NOST7629 |

Note: the above titles are radio broadcasts from the "Downbeat Club".

Same as July-August, 1947. *NYC. August 22, 1947.*

| | | |
|---|---|---|
| D7VB 1542 | OW | RCA (Eu) PM42408 |
| D7VB 1543 | OOP-POP-A-DA vcl DG, KH | RCA (Eu) PM42408 |
| D7VB 1544 | TWO BASS HIT | RCA (Eu) PM42408 |
| D7VB 1545 | STAY ON IT | RCA (Eu) PM42408 |

### DIZZY GILLESPIE AND HIS ORCHESTRA

Dizzy Gillespie (tp, vcl); Dave Burns, Benny Bailey, Lamar Wright jr, Elmon Wright (tp); Ted Kelly, Bill Shepherd (tb); John Brown, Howard Johnson (as); George 'Big Nick' Nicholas, Joe Gayles (ts); Cecil Payne (bars); John Lewis (p); Al McKibbon (b); Kenny Clarke (d); Chano Pozo (conga, vcl); Kenny Hagood (vcl). *NYC. December 22, 1947.*

| | | |
|---|---|---|
| 47VB 2933 | COOL BREEZE vcl DG, KH | RCA (Eu) PM42408 |
| 47VB 2934 | CUBANA BE | RCA (Eu) PM42408 |
| 47VB 2935 | CUBANA BOP | RCA (Eu) PM42408 |

Sames as December 22, 1947. *NYC. December 30, 1947.*

| | | |
|---|---|---|
| 47VB 3090 | MANTECA | RCA (Eu) PM42408 |
| 47VB 3092 | GOOD BAIT | RCA (Eu) PM42408 |
| 47VB 3093 | OOL-YA-KOO vcl DG, KH | RCA (Eu) PM42408 |
| 47VB 3094 | MINOR WALK | RCA (Eu) PM42408 |

Same as December 22, 1947. *Stockholm, Sweden. February 2, 1948.*

| | |
|---|---|
| THEME (I waited for you) | Dragon (Eu) DRLP34 |

# DIZZY GILLESPIE

## A SELECTIVE DISCOGRAPHY

| | |
|---|---|
| OUR DELIGHT | Dragon (Eu) DRLP34 |
| I CAN'T GET STARTED | Dragon (Eu) DRLP34 |
| OOL-YA-KOO | Dragon (Eu) DRLP34 |
| MANTECA | Dragon (Eu) DRLP34 |
| MORE THAN YOU KNOW | Dragon (Eu) DRLP34 |
| OO-POP-A-DA | Dragon (Eu) DRLP34 |
| RAY'S IDEA | Dragon (Eu) DRLP34 |
| THEME (I waited for you) | Dragon (Eu) DRLP34 |

Note: other titles on DRLP34 do not feature Dizzy Gillespie.


Same as December 22, 1947. *Paris, France. February 28, 1948.*

| | |
|---|---|
| 'ROUND ABOUT MIDNIGHT | Jazz Reactivation (Eu) JR141 |
| ALGO BUENO | Jazz Reactivation (Eu) JR141 |
| I CAN'T GET STARTED | Jazz Reactivation (Eu) JR141 |
| OOL-YA-KOO vcl DG, KH | Jazz Reactivation (Eu) JR141 |
| AFRO CUBAN SUITE | Jazz Reactivation (Eu) JR141 |
| OOP-POP-A-DA vcl DG, KH | Jazz Reactivation (Eu) JR141 |
| TWO BASS HIT | Jazz Reactivation (Eu) JR141 |
| GOOD BAIT | Jazz Reactivation (Eu) JR141 |
| THINGS TO COME | Jazz Reactivation (Eu) JR141 |


**DIZZY GILLESPIE AND HIS ORCHESTRA**

Dizzy Gillespie (tp, vcl); Dave Burns, Willie Cook, Elmon Wright (tp). Andy Duryea, Sam Hurt, Jesse Tarrant (tb); John Brown, Ernie Henry (as); Budd Johnson, Joe Gayles (ts); Cecil Payne (bars); James Forman (piano, celeste); Al McKibbon (b); Teddy Stewart (d); Sabu Martinez (bongos); Joe Harris (conga). *NYC. December 28, 1948.*

# DIZZY GILLESPIE

## A SELECTIVE DISCOGRAPHY

| | | |
|---|---|---|
| D8VB 4148 – 1 | GUARACHI GUARO | RCA (Eu) PM42408 |
| D8VB 4149 – 1 | DUFF CAPERS | RCA (Eu) PM42408 |
| D8VB 4150 – 1 | LOVER COME BACK TO ME | RCA (Eu) PM42408 |
| D8VB 4151 – 1 | I'M BE BOPPIN' TOO vcl DG | RCA (Eu) PM42408 |
| D8VB 4151 – 2 | I'M BE BOPPIN' TOO vcl DG | RCA (Eu) PM42408 |

Note: Dizzy Gillespie recorded with the Metronome All Stars, RCA records, NYC January 3, 1949. Two titles issued on PM42408.

Same as December 28, 1948 except Benny Harris (tp), Yusef Lateef (ts), Al Gibson (bars) and Vince Guerra (conga) replace Dave Burns, Budd Johnson, Cecil Payne and Joe Harris. Omit Sabu Martinez, add Joe Carroll (vcl). *NYC. April 14, 1949.*

| | | |
|---|---|---|
| D9VB 471 | SWEDISH SUITE | RCA (Eu) PM42408 |
| D9VB 472 – 1 | ST. LOUIS BLUES | RCA (Eu) PM42408 |

Same as April 14, 1949. *NYC. May 6, 1949.*

| | | |
|---|---|---|
| D9VB 1010 – 1 | KATY (Dizzier and Dizzier) | RCA (Eu) PM42408 |
| D9VB 1011 – 1 | JUMP DID-LE-BA vcl DG, JC | RCA (Eu) PM42408 |

Same as April 14, 1949 except J. J. Johnson, Charles Greenlea (tb) replace Sam Hurt and Jesse Tarrant. *NYC. July 6, 1949.*

| | | |
|---|---|---|
| D9VB 1793 – 1 | HEY PETE vcl DG, JC | RCA (Eu) PM42408 |
| D9VB 1794 – 1 | JUMPIN' WITH SYMPHONY SID | RCA (Eu) PM42408 |
| D9VB 1796 – 1 | IN THE LAND OF OO-BLA-DEE | |
| | vcl JC | RCA (Eu) PM42408 |

# DIZZY GILLESPIE
## A SELECTIVE DISCOGRAPHY

### DIZZY GILLESPIE SEXTET

Dizzy Gillespie (tp, vcl); Jimmy Heath (as); Jimmy Oliver (ts); Milt Jackson (p); Percy Heath (b); Joe Harris (d). *NYC. September 16, 1950.*

| 108 | SHE'S GONE AGAIN vcl DG and band | Prestige (Eu) PR24030 |
| 109 | NICE WORK IF YOU CAN GET IT | Prestige (Eu) PR24030 |
| 110 | THINKING OF YOU | Prestige (Eu) PR24030 |

### DIZZY GILLESPIE with Johnny Richards Orchestra

Dizzy Gillespie (tp, vcl); Dick Kenny, Henry Coker, Harold Smith (tb). John Graas (frh); 6 strings; 4 woodwinds; harp; Paul Smith (p); Jack Cascales (b); Specs Wright (d); Carlos Vidal (latin percussion); Johnny Richards (arr, cond). *LA. October 30, 1950.*

| D385 | SWING LOW SWEET CHARIOT | |
| | vcl DG and ensemble | Savoy (Am) SJL2254 |
| D386 | LULLABY OF THE LEAVES | Savoy (Am) SJL2254 |
| D387 | MILLION DOLLAR BABY | Savoy (Am) SJL2254 |
| D388 | WHAT IS THERE TO SAY | Savoy (Am) SJL2254 |

Same as October 30, 1950. *LA. November 1, 1950.*

| D389 | ALONE TOGETHER | Savoy (Am) SJL2254 |
| D390 | THESE ARE THE THINGS I LOVE | Savoy (Am) SJL2254 |
| D391 | ON THE ALAMO | Savoy (Am) SJL2254 |
| D392 | INTERLUDE | Savoy (Am) SJL2254 |

Note: other titles on SJL2254 do not feature Dizzy Gillespie.

# DIZZY GILLESPIE

## A SELECTIVE DISCOGRAPHY

### DIZZY GILLESPIE SEXTET

Dizzy Gillespie (tp); John Coltrane (as, ts); Milt Jackson (p, vbs); Kenny Burrell (g); Percy Heath (b); Kansas Fields (d); The Calypso Boys (maracas, bongos); Freddy Strong (vcl). *Detroit. March 1, 1951.*

| 4010 | WE LOVE TO BOOGIE vcl FS | Savoy (Am) SJL2209 |
| 4015 | TIN TIN DEO | Savoy (Am) SJL2209 |
| 4020 | BIRK'S WORKS | Savoy (Am) SJL2209 |

### DIZZY GILLESPIE SEXTET

Dizzy Gillespie (tp. p-1); J. J. Johnson (tb); Budd Johnson (ts); Milt Jackson (p, vbs); Percy Heath (b); Art Blakey (d); Joe Carroll, Melvin Moore (vcl). *NYC. April 16, 1951.*

| 3636 | LADY BE GOOD vcl JC | Savoy (Am) SJL2209 |
| 3637 | LOVE ME PRETTY BABY vcl MM | Savoy (Am) SJL2209 |
| 3638 | THE CHAMP parts 1 & 2 −1 | Savoy (Am) SJL2209 |

### DIZZY GILLESPIE SEXTET

Dizzy Gillespie (tp, vcl); Bill Graham (bars); Milt Jackson (p, vbs); Percy Heath (b); Al Jones (d); unknown latin percussion − 1; Joe Carroll, Melvin Moore (vcl). *NYC. August 16, 1951.*

| 1206 | I'M IN A MESS vcl JC | Savoy (Am) SJL2209 |
| 1210 | SCHOOL DAYS vcl JC | Savoy (Am) SJL2209 |
| 1500 | SWING LOW SWEET CADILLAC | |
| | vcl DG and ensemble  −1 | Savoy (Am) SJL2209 |
| | BOPSIE'S BLUES vcl MM | Savoy (Am) SJL2209 |
| | BOPSIE'S BLUES vcl MM | |
| | (alternate take) | Savoy (Am) SJL2209 |

# DIZZY GILLESPIE

## A SELECTIVE DISCOGRAPHY

I COULDN'T BEAT THE RAP
  vcl MM                                    Savoy (Am) SJL2209

**DIZZY GILLESPIE SEXTET**

Dizzy Gillespie (tp, vcl); Bill Graham (bars); Stuff Smith (violin) −1; Milt Jackson (p, vcl); Percy Heath (b); Al Jones (d); Joe Carroll (vcl). *NYC. October 25, 1951.*

| | | |
|---|---|---|
| 2300 | CARAVAN −1 | Savoy (Am) SJL2209 |
| 2300 | CARAVAN −1 (alternate take) | Savoy (Am) SJL2209 |
| 2301 | NOBODY KNOWS vcl JC and ensemble | Savoy (Am) SJL2209 |
| 2302 | THE BLUEST BLUES vcl JC | Savoy (Am) SJL2209 |
| 2303 | ON THE SUNNY SIDE OF THE STREET vcl DG, JC −1 | Savoy (Am) SJL2209 |
| 2304 | STARDUST −1 | Savoy (Am) SJL2209 |
| 2305 | TIME ON MY HANDS vcl MJ | Savoy (Am) SJL2209 |

Note: latin percussion heard on CARAVAN. Dizzy Gillespie or Milt Jackson play organ on TIME ON MY HANDS.

**DIZZY GILLESPIE QUINTET**

Dizzy Gillespie (tp, vcl); Bill Graham (bars); Wynton Kelly (p); Bernie Griggs (b); Al Jones (d); Joe Carroll (vcl). *NYC. July 18, 1952.*

| | | |
|---|---|---|
| 2306 | BLUE SKIES | Savoy (Am) SJL2209 |
| 2307 | UMBRELLA MAN vcl JC and ensemble | Savoy (Am) SJL2209 |
| 2308 | POP'S CONFESSIN' vcl DG | Savoy (Am) SJL2209 |
| 2309 | OO-SHOO-BE-DOO-BE vcl DG, JC | Savoy (Am) SJL2209 |
| | THEY CAN'T TAKE THAT AWAY FROM ME | Savoy (Am) SJL2209 |

# DIZZY GILLESPIE

## A SELECTIVE DISCOGRAPHY

**DIZZY GILLESPIE SEXTET**

Dizzy Gillespie (tp, vcl); Bill Graham (bars); Wade Legge (p); Lou Hackney (b); Al Jones (d); Joe Carroll (vcl, maracas). *Paris, France. February 9, 1953.*

| | |
|---|---|
| THE CHAMP vcl DG, JC | Jazz Reactivation (Eu) JR 137 |
| OO-SHOO-BE-DOO-BE vcl DG, JC | Jazz Reactivation (Eu) JR 137 |
| THEY CAN'T TAKE THAT AWAY FROM ME | Jazz Reactivation (Eu) JR 137 |
| GOOD BAIT | Jazz Reactivation (Eu) JR 137 |
| SUNNY SIDE OF THE STREET vcl DG, JC | Jazz Reactivation (Eu) JR 137 |
| SWING LOW SWEET CADILLAC vcl DG and ensemble | Jazz Reactivation (Eu) JR 137 |
| THE BLUEST BLUES vcl JC | Jazz Reactivation (Eu) JR 137 |
| SCHOOL DAYS vcl JC | Jazz Reactivation (Eu) JR 137 |
| BIRK'S WORKS | Jazz Reactivation (Eu) JR 137 |
| TIN TIN DEO | Jazz Reactivation (Eu) JR 137 |

Note: the above titles taken from a concert at Salle Pleyel, Paris. Dizzy Gillespie conga on SWING LOW SWEET CADILLAC and TIN TIN DEO.

**DIZZY GILLESPIE-STAN GETZ SEXTET**

Dizzy Gillespie (tp); Stan Getz (ts); Oscar Peterson (p); Herb Ellis (g); Ray Brown (b); Max Roach (d). *LA. December 9, 1953.*

| | | |
|---|---|---|
| 1367 – 3 | GIRL OF MY DREAMS | Verve (Eu) 2610045 |
| 1368 – 7 | IT DON'T MEAN A THING IF IT AIN'T GOT THAT SWING | Verve (Eu) 2610045 |
| 1369 – 1 | IT'S THE TALK OF THE TOWN | Verve (Eu) 2610045 |
| 1370 – 2 | SIBONEY pt 1 | Verve (Eu) 2610045 |
| 1371 – 2 | SIBONEY pt 2 | Verve (Eu) 2610045 |
| 1372 – 3 | EXACTLY LIKE YOU | Verve (Eu) 2610045 |
| 1373 – 3 | I LET A SONG GO OUT OF | |

# DIZZY GILLESPIE
## A SELECTIVE DISCOGRAPHY

|  | MY HEART | Verve (Eu) 2610045 |
| 1374 – 1 | IMPROMPTU | Verve (Eu) 2610045 |

### DIZZY GILLESPIE BIG BAND

Dizzy Gillespie, Quincy Jones, Ernie Royal, Jimmy Nottingham (tp); Leon Comegyes, J. J. Johnson, George Matthews (tb); Hilton Jefferson, George Dorsey (as); Hank Mobley, Lucky Thompson (ts); Danny Bank (bars); Wade Legge (p); Lou Hackney (b); Charlie Persip (d); Buster Harding (arr). *NYC. September 15, 1954.*

| 1980 – 3 | COOL EYES | Verve (J) MV2671 |
| 1981 – 1 | CONFUSION | Verve (J) MV2671 |
| 1982 – 2 | PILE DRIVER | Verve (J) MV2671 |
| 1983 – 2 | HOB NAIL SPECIAL | Verve (J) MV2671 |

### DIZZY GILLESPIE with Johnny Richards Orchestra

Dizzy Gillespie (tp, vcl); John Barrows, Jimmy Buffington, Jim Chambers, Fred Klein (frh); George Berg, Jack Greenberg, Tom Parshley (woodwinds); Danny Bank (bars); Wynton Kelly (p); Percy Heath (b); Jimmy Crawford (d); Johnny Richards (arr, cond). *NYC. September 16, 1954.*

| 1984 | ROSES OF PICARDY | Verve (J) MV2671 |
| 1985 | SILHOUETTE | Verve (J) MV2671 |
| 1986 | CAN YOU RECALL? | Verve (J) MV2671 |
| 1987 | O SOLOW vcl DG | Verve (J) MV2671 |

# DIZZY GILLESPIE

## A SELECTIVE DISCOGRAPHY

### DIZZY GILLESPIE WITH THE ORCHESTRA

Dizzy Gillespie (tp, vcl); Ed Leddy, Marky Markowitz, Bob Carey, Charlie Frankhauser, Bunny Aldhizer, Al Porcino (tp); Earl Swope, Rob Swope, Dick Leith (tb); Mike Goldberg (as); Angelo Tompros, Jim Parker, Spencer Sinatra (ts); Joel Davie (bars); Larry Eanet (p); Ed Diamond (p, percussion); Mert Oliver, Tom McKay (b); Joe Timer (d); Jack Franklin (percussion); Buddy Rowell (timbales); "Bovino", George Caldwell (congas). *Washington, D.C. March 3, 1955.*

|  |  |
|---|---|
| THE AFRO SUITE | Electra (Eu) 96 – 0300 – 1 |
| HOBNAIL BOOGIE | Electra (Eu) 96 – 0300 – 1 |
| WILD BILL'S BOOGIE | Electra (Eu) 96 – 0300 – 1 |
| CARAVAN | Electra (Eu) 96 – 0300 – 1 |
| TIN TIN DEO | Electra (Eu) 96 – 0300 – 1 |
| UP 'N' DOWNS | Electra (Eu) 96 – 0300 – 1 |

Note: the above titles recorded at Club Kavakos, Washington. Personnel here is collective; further details contained in LP sleeve notes.

### DIZZY GILLESPIE AND HIS ORCHESTRA

Dizzy Gillespie (tp, vcl, arr); Quincy Jones (tp, arr); Joe Gordon, Carl Warwick, Ermet Perry (tp); Melba Liston (tb, arr); Rod Levitt, Frank Rehak (tb); Jimmy Powell, Phil Woods (as); Billy Mitchell (ts); Ernie Wilkins (ts, arr); Marty Flax (bars); Walter Davis jr (p); Nelson Boyd (b); Charlie Persip (d); A. K. Salim (arr). *NYC. June 6, 1956.*

| | | |
|---|---|---|
| 2831 – 1 | DIZZY'S BUSINESS arr EW | Verve (J) MV2590 |
| 2832 – 2 | HEY PETE vcl DG and band | Verve (J) MV2630 |
| 2833 – 1 | JESSICA'S DAY arr QJ | Verve (J) MV2590 |
| 2834 – 1 | TOUR DE FORCE arr DG | Verve (J) MV2590 |
| 2835 – 1 | I CAN'T GET STARTED | |
| | arr QJ | Verve (J) MV2590 |

| 2836 – 3 | STELLA BY STARLIGHT arr ML | Verve (J) MV2590 |
|---|---|---|
| 2837 – 1 | DOODLIN' | Verve (J) MV2590 |
| 2838 – 1 | NIGHT IN TUNISIA | Verve (J) MV2590 |
| 2839 – 1 | THE CHAMP arr QJ | Verve (J) MV2590 |
| 2840 – 1 | YESTERDAYS | Verve (J) MV2630 |
| 2841 – 2 | TIN TIN DEO | Verve (J) MV2630 |
| 2842 – 2 | GROOVIN' FOR NAT arr EW | Verve (J) MV2630 |
| 2843 – 1 | MY REVERIE arr ML | Verve (J) MV2590 |
| 2844 – 1 | DIZZY'S BLUES arr AKS | Verve (J) MV2590 |
| 2845 – 2 | ANNIE'S DANCE arr ML | Verve (J) MV2630 |
| 2846 – 2 | COOL BREEZE | Verve (J) MV2630 |
| 2847 – 2 | SCHOOL DAYS vcl DG, arr QJ | Verve (J) MV2630 |

Same as June 6, 1956; add Austin Cromer (vcl). *NYC. June, 1956.*

| Theme and intro | Fanfare (Am) LP No. 46 – 146 |
|---|---|
| DIZZY'S BLUES arr AKS | Fanfare (Am) LP No. 46 – 146 |
| NIGHT IN TUNISIA | Fanfare (Am) LP No. 46 – 146 |
| STELLA BY STARLIGHT arr ML | Fanfare (Am) LP No. 46 – 146 |
| DOODLIN' | Fanfare (Am) LP No. 46 – 146 |
| IF YOU COULD SEE ME NOW vcl AC | Fanfare (Am) LP No. 46 – 146 |
| GROVIN' FOR NAT arr EW | Fanfare (Am) LP No. 46 – 146 |
| WHISPER NOT | Fanfare (Am) LP No. 46 – 146 |
| TANGERINE | Fanfare (Am) LP No. 46 – 146 |
| DIZZY'S BUSINESS arr EW | Fanfare (Am) LP No. 46 – 146 |

Note: my list of personnel differs slightly from the sleeve of 46 – 146 and is thought to be more accurate. Recordings taken from radio broadcasts.

# DIZZY GILLESPIE

## A SELECTIVE DISCOGRAPHY

### DIZZY GILLESPIE AND HIS ORCHESTRA

Dizzy Gillespie (tp, vcl, arr); Lee Morgan, Carl Warwick, Talib Daawood, Ermet Perry (tp); Melba Liston (tb, arr); Chuck Connor, Al Grey (tb); Jimmy Powell, Ernie Henry (as); Billy Mitchell (ts); Benny Golson (ts, arr); Pee Wee Moore (bars); Wynton Kelly (p); Paul West (b); Charlie Persip (d); Mary Lou Williams (p) – 1; Ernie Wilkins, A. K. Salim, Quincy Jones, Tadd Dameron (arr). *Rhode Island. July 6, 1957.*

| | |
|---|---|
| DIZZY'S BLUES arr AKS | Verve (Eu) 2304348 |
| DOODLIN' arr EW | Verve (Eu) 2304348 |
| SCHOOLDAYS vcl DG arr QJ | Verve (Eu) 2304348 |
| I REMEMBER CLIFFORD arr BG | Verve (Eu) 2304348 |
| COOL BREEZE arr TD | Verve (Eu) 2304348 |
| MANTECA arr DG | Verve (J) MV2620 |
| ZODIAC SUITE – 1 | Verve (J) MV2620 |
| CARIOCA – 1 | Verve (J) MV2620 |

Note: the above recording took place at the Newport Jazz Festival. Other titles on MV2620 do not feature Dizzy Gillespie.

### DIZZY GILLESPIE OCTET

Dizzy Gillespie (tp); Henry Coker (tb); Gigi Gryce (as, arr); Benny Golson (ts, arr); Pee Wee Moore (bars); Ray Bryant (p). Tom Bryant (b); Charlie Persip (d). *NYC. December 17, 1957.*

| | | |
|---|---|---|
| 21849 | BLUES AFTER DARK | Verve (Eu) 2304382 |
| 21850 | SEABREEZE | Verve (Eu) 2304382 |
| 21851 | OUT OF THE PAST | Verve (Eu) 2304382 |

# DIZZY GILLESPIE

## A SELECTIVE DISCOGRAPHY

| | | |
|---|---|---|
| 21852 | SHABOZZ | Verve (Eu) 2304382 |
| 21853 | REMINISCING | Verve (Eu) 2304382 |
| 21854 | A NITE AT TONY'S | Verve (Eu) 2304382 |
| 21855 | SMOKE SIGNALS | Verve (Eu) 2304382 |
| 21856 | JUST BY MYSELF | Verve (Eu) 2304382 |

**DIZZY GILLESPIE QUINTET**

Dizzy Gillespie (tp); Les Spann (fl, g); Junior Mance (p); Sam Jones (b); Lex Humphries (d). *NYC. February 17, 1959.*

| | | |
|---|---|---|
| 22712 – 5 | MY MAN | Verve (J) MV2696 |
| 22713 – 3 | MOONGLOW | Verve (J) MV2696 |
| 22714 – 5 | THERE IS NO GREATER LOVE | Verve (J) MV2696 |
| 22716 – 2 | ST. LOUIS BLUES | Verve (J) MV2696 |

Same as February 17, 1959. *NYC. February 18, 1959.*

| | | |
|---|---|---|
| 22717 – 5 | MILLION DOLLAR BABY | Verve (J) MV2696 |
| 22722 – 1 | MY HEART BELONGS TO DADDY | Verve (J) MV2696 |

Same as February 17, 1959. *NYC. February 20, 1959.*

| | | |
|---|---|---|
| 22724 – 1 | WRAP YOUR TROUBLES IN DREAMS | Verve (J) MV2696 |
| 22725 – 2 | WOODY 'N' YOU | Verve (J) MV2696 |

# DIZZY GILLESPIE

## A SELECTIVE DISCOGRAPHY

**DIZZY GILLESPIE QUINTET**

Dizzy Gillespie (tp, vcl); Leo Wright (as, fl); Lalo Schifrin (p); Bob Cunningham (b); Chuck Lampkin (d). *NYC. February 9, 1961.*

| | |
|---|---|
| KUSH | Verve (J) MV2605 |
| SALT PEANUTS vcl DG | Verve (J) MV2605 |
| A NIGHT IN TUNISIA | Verve (J) MV2605 |
| THE MOOCHE | Verve (J) MV2605 |

Note: the above titles recorded in concert at the Museum of Modern Art, NY.

**DIZZY GILLESPIE QUINTET**

Dizzy Gillespie (tp); James Moody (as, ts, fl); Kenny Barron (p); Chris White (b); Rudy Collins (d). *NYC. April 23, 1963.*

| 22934 | BE BOP | Mercury (Eu) 6336304 |
|---|---|---|
| 22935 | GOOD BAIT | Mercury (Eu) 6336304 |

Same as April 23, 1963. *NYC. April 24, 1963.*

| 22950 | I CAN'T GET STARTED/ ROUND MIDNIGHT | Mercury (Eu) 6336304 |
|---|---|---|

Same as April 23, 1963. *NYC. April 25, 1963.*

| 22955 | DIZZY ATMOSPHERE | Mercury (Eu) 6336304 |
|---|---|---|
| 22956 | THE CUP BEARERS | Mercury (Eu) 6336304 |

# DIZZY GILLESPIE

## A SELECTIVE DISCOGRAPHY

| | | |
|---|---|---|
| 22957 | THE DAY AFTER | Mercury (Eu) 6336304 |
| 22958 | NOVEMBER AFTERNOON | Mercury (Eu) 6336304 |
| 22959 | THIS LOVELY EVENING | Mercury (Eu) 6336304 |

## DIZZY GILLESPIE AND THE DOUBLE SIX

Dizzy Gillespie (tp); Bud Powell (p); Pierre Michelot (b); Kenny Clarke (d). *Paris, France. June/July, 1963.*

| | | |
|---|---|---|
| 29173 | ONE BASS HIT | Phillips (Eu) 6337203 |
| 29174 | TWO BASS HIT | Phillips (Eu) 6337203 |
| 29175 | EMANON | Phillips (Eu) 6337203 |
| 29176 | BLUE 'N' BOOGIE | Phillips (Eu) 6337203 |
| 29177 | THE CHAMP | Phillips (Eu) 6337203 |
| 29178 | TIN TIN DEO | Phillips (Eu) 6337203 |
| 29179 | GROOVIN' HIGH | Phillips (Eu) 6337203 |
| 29180 | OW | Phillips (Eu) 6337203 |
| 29181 | HOT HOUSE | Phillips (Eu) 6337203 |
| 29182 | ANTHROPOLOGY | Phillips (Eu) 6337203 |

Dizzy Gillespie (tp); James Moody (ts, fl); Kenny Barron (p); Chris White (b); Rudy Collins (d). *Chicago. September 20, 1963.*

| | | |
|---|---|---|
| 29358 | CON ALMA | Phillips (Eu) 6337203 |
| 29359 | OO-SHOO-BE-DOO | Phillips (Eu) 6337203 |

Note: The Double Six – Mimi Perrin, Claudine Barge, Christine Legrand, Ward Swingle, Robert Smart, Jean-Claude Briodin and Eddy Louis vocals, dubbed over music tracks at a later date. Vocal arrangements by Lalo Schifrin.

# DIZZY GILLESPIE

## A SELECTIVE DISCOGRAPHY

### DIZZY GILLESPIE QUINTET

Dizzy Gillespie (tp, vcl); James Moody (as, ts, fl, vcl); Mike Longo (p); Frank Schifano (b); Candy Finch (d). *LA. May 25/26, 1967.*

| | |
|---|---|
| SWING LOW SWEET CADILLAC | |
| vcl DG, JM | Jasmine (Eu) JAS5 |
| MAS QUE | Jasmine (Eu) JAS5 |
| BYE | Jasmine (Eu) JAS5 |
| SOMETHING IN YOUR SMILE vcl DG | Jasmine (Eu) JAS5 |
| KUSH | Jasmine (Eu) JAS5 |

Note: the above titles recorded at Memory Lane Club.

### THE DIZZY GILLESPIE REUNION BIG BAND

Dizzy Gillespie, Jimmy Owens, Dizzy Reece, Victor Paz, Stu Hamier (tp); Curtis Fuller, Tom McIntosh, Ted Kelly (tb); Chris Woods (as); James Moody (ts, fl); Paul Jeffrey (ts); Sahib Shihab, Cecil Payne (bars); Mike Longo (p); Paul West (b); Candy Finch (d). *W. Germany. November 7, 1968.*

| | |
|---|---|
| THINGS TO COME | MPS (Eu) 15207 |
| ONE BASS HIT | MPS (Eu) 15207 |
| FRISCO | MPS (Eu) 15207 |
| CON ALMA | MPS (Eu) 15207 |
| THE THINGS ARE HERE | MPS (Eu) 15207 |
| THEME (Birk's Works) | MPS (Eu) 15207 |

Note: the above titles recorded at Berlin Philharmonic Hall.

# DIZZY GILLESPIE
## A SELECTIVE DISCOGRAPHY

**DIZZY GILLESPIE**

Dizzy Gillespie (tp); Mike Longo (p); George Davis (g); Andrew Gonzalez (b); Jerry Gonzalez (conga); Nicholas Marrero (timbales); Carlos Valdez (conga). *NYC. January, 1971.*

| | |
|---|---|
| OLINGA | Festival (Eu) 215 |
| DIDDY WA DIDDY | Festival (Eu) 215 |
| ME 'N' THEM | Festival (Eu) 215 |
| TIMET | Festival (Eu) 215 |

**DIZZY GILLESPIE**

Dizzy Gillespie, Bobby Hackett (tp); Mary Lou Williams (p); George Duvivier (b); Grady Tate (d). *NYC. January 31, 1971.*

| | |
|---|---|
| LOVE FOR SALE | Festival (Eu) 215 |
| AUTUMN LEAVES | Festival (Eu) 215 |
| CARAVAN | Festival (Eu) 215 |
| JITTERBUG WALTZ | Festival (Eu) 215 |
| WILLOW WEEP FOR ME | Festival (Eu) 215 |
| BIRK'S WORKS | Festival (Eu) 215 |
| MY MAN | Festival (Eu) 215 |

Note: the above recordings are from a concert at The Overseas Press Club, New York.

# DIZZY GILLESPIE

## A SELECTIVE DISCOGRAPHY

### DIZZY GILLESPIE AND THE MITCHELL RUFF TRIO

Dizzy Gillespie (tp); Dwike Mitchell (p); Willie Ruff (b, frh). *New Hampshire. 1971*

| | |
|---|---|
| CON ALMA | Mainstream (Eu) MRL5004 |
| DARTMOUTH DUET | Mainstream (Eu) MRL5004 |
| WOODY 'N YOU | Mainstream (Eu) MRL5004 |
| BLUES PEOPLE | Mainstream (Eu) MRL5004 |
| BELLA BELLA | Mainstream (Eu) MRL5004 |

Note: the above recordings are from a concert at Dartmouth College, Hanover.

### DIZZY GILLESPIE SEXTET

Dizzy Gillespie (tp); Johnny Griffin (ts); Kenny Drew (p); N. H. O. Pedersen (b); Kenny Clarke (d); Humberto Canto (timbales). *Paris, France. April, 1973.*

| | |
|---|---|
| MANTECA | America (Eu) 30 AM6135 |
| ALONE TOGETHER | America (Eu) 30 AM6135 |
| BROTHER 'K' | America (Eu) 30 AM6135 |
| WHEATLEIGH HALL | America (Eu) 30 AM6135 |
| STELLA BY STARLIGHT | America (Eu) 30 AM6133 |
| I WAITED FOR YOU | America (Eu) 30 AM6133 |
| FIESTA MO-JO | America (Eu) 30 AM6133 |
| SERENITY | America (Eu) 30 AM6133 |

# DIZZY GILLESPIE

## A SELECTIVE DISCOGRAPHY

**DIZZY GILLESPIE BIG FOUR**

Dizzy Gillespie (tp); Joe Pass (g); Ray Brown (b); Micky Roker (d). *LA. September 19, 1974.*

| | |
|---|---|
| TENGA | Pablo 2310719 |
| HURRY HOME | Pablo 2310719 |
| RUSSIAN LULLABY | Pablo 2310719 |
| BEBOP (Dizzy Fingers) | Pablo 2310719 |
| BIRK'S WORKS | Pablo 2310719 |
| SEPTEMBER SONG | Pablo 2310719 |
| JITTERBUG WALTZ | Pablo 2310719 |

**GILLESPIEZ-PETERSON DUO**

Dizzy Gillespie (tp); Oscar Peterson (p). *London, England. November 28-29, 1974.*

| | |
|---|---|
| CARAVAN | Pablo 2310740 |
| MOZAMBIQUE | Pablo 2310740 |
| AUTUMN LEAVES | Pablo 2310740 |
| CLOSE YOUR EYES | Pablo 2310740 |
| BLUES FOR BIRD | Pablo 2310740 |
| DIZZY ATMOSPHERE | Pablo 2310740 |
| ALONE TOGETHER | Pablo 2310740 |
| CON ALMA | Pablo 2310740 |
| STELLA BY STARLIGHT | Pablo 2310817 |
| THERE IS NO GREATER LOVE | Pablo 2310817 |

Note: other tracks on 2310817 do not feature Dizzy Gillespie.

# DIZZY GILLESPIE

## A SELECTIVE DISCOGRAPHY

**DIZZY GILLESPIE Y MACHITO**

Dizzy Gillespie (tp); Victor Paz, Paul Gonzalez, Ramon Gonzalez jr, Manny Duran (tp, flh); Barry Morrow, Lewis Kahn, Gerald Chamberlain (tb); Brooks Tillotson, Don Corrado (frh); Bob Stewart (tu); Mario Bauza (as, cl); Mauricio Smith (as, fl, piccolo); Jose Madera (ts, cl); Mario Rivera (ts, alto fl); Jorge Dalto (electric p); Carlos Castillo (b); Dana McCurdy (synthesizer); Micky Roker (d); Julio Colazo, Rene Hernandez (African d); Mario Grillo (bongos, congas, bells, percussion). Jose Madera jr (timbales, cabassa, percussion); Machito (maracas, claves). *NYC. June 4-5, 1975.*

| | |
|---|---|
| ORO INCENSIO Y MIRRA | Pablo 2310771 |
| CA LIDOSCOPICO | Pablo 2310771 |
| PENSATIVO | Pablo 2310771 |
| EXUBERANTE | Pablo 2310771 |

**DIZZY GILLESPIE BIG SEVEN**

Dizzy Gillespie (tp); Eddie Davis, Johnny Griffin (ts); Milt Jackson (vbs); Tommy Flanagan (p); N. H. O. Pedersen (b); Louis Bellson (d). *Switzerland. July 16, 1975.*

| | |
|---|---|
| LOVER COME BACK TO ME | Pablo 2310749 |
| WHAT'S NEW | Pablo 2310749 |
| CHEROKEE | Pablo 2310749 |
| I'LL REMEMBER APRIL | Pablo 2625707 |

Note: the above titles recorded at the Montreux Jazz Festival.

# DIZZY GILLESPIE
## A SELECTIVE DISCOGRAPHY

**DIZZY GILLESPIE ORCHESTRA**

Dizzy Gillespie (tp); Roger Glenn (fl, bass fl, vbs); Al Gaffa, Mike Howell (g); Earl May (b); Micky Roker (d); Paulo Paulinho (percussion). *November 19/20, 1975.*

| | |
|---|---|
| CARNIVA | Pablo 2625708 |
| SAMBA | Pablo 2625708 |
| BARCELONA | Pablo 2625708 |
| IN THE LAND OF THE LIVING DEAD | Pablo 2625708 |
| BEHIND THE MOONBEAM | Pablo 2625708 |
| THE TRUTH | Pablo 2625708 |
| PELE | Pablo 2625708 |
| OLINGA | Pablo 2625708 |

**DIZZY GILLESPIE-BENNY CARTER**

Dizzy Gillespie (tp); Benny Carter (as); Tommy Flanagan (p); Joe Pass (g); Al McGibbon (b); Micky Roker (d, vcl). *April 27, 1976.*

| | |
|---|---|
| SWEET AND LOVELY | Pablo 2310781 |
| BROADWAY | Pablo 2310781 |
| THE COURTSHIP | Pablo 2310781 |
| CONSTANTINOPLE | Pablo 2310781 |
| NOBODY KNOWS THE TROUBLE I'VE SEEN | Pablo 2310781 |
| NIGHT IN TUNISIA | Pablo 2310781 |

# DIZZY GILLESPIE

A SELECTIVE DISCOGRAPHY

**DIZZY GILLESPIE SEXTET**

Dizzy Gillespie (tp); Ray Pizzi (ts, sop fl); Rodney Jones (g); Benjamin Franklin Brown (b); Micky Roker (d); Paulino DaCosta (percussion). *September 15/16, 1976.*

| | |
|---|---|
| DIZZY'S PARTY | Pablo 2310784 |
| SHIM-SHAM SHIMMY ON THE | |
| ST. LOUIS BLUES | Pablo 2310784 |
| HARLEM SAMBA | Pablo 2310784 |
| LAND OF MILK AND HONEY | Pablo 2310784 |

**DIZZY GILLESPIE with Lalo Schifrin Orchestra**
Dizzy Gillespie, Oscar Brashear, Jack Laubach (tp); Lew McCreary (tb); James Horn, Ernie Watts, Jerome Richardson (saxs, fl); Sonny Burke (fender rhodes, p); Ray Parker jr; Lee Ritenour, Wa Wa Watson (g); Wilton Fender (b); Edward Greene (d); Paulino Da Costa (percussion); Lalo Schifrin (keyboards, arr, cond). *LA. January 31, February 1 and 2, 1977.*

| | |
|---|---|
| UNICORN | Pablo 2310794 |
| FIRE DANCE | Pablo 2310794 |
| INCANTATION | Pablo 2310794 |
| WRONG NUMBER | Pablo 2310794 |
| FREE RIDE | Pablo 2310794 |
| OZONE MADNESS | Pablo 2310794 |
| LOVE POEM FOR DONNA | Pablo 2310794 |
| THE LAST STROKE OF | |
| MIDNIGHT | Pablo 2310794 |

# DIZZY GILLESPIE
## A SELECTIVE DISCOGRAPHY

**DIZZY GILLESPIE-COUNT BASIE**

Dizzy Gillespie (tp); Count Basie (p); Ray Brown (b); Mickey Roker (d). *Las Vegas. February 3, 1977.*

| | |
|---|---|
| BACK TO THE LAND | Pablo 2310833 |
| CONSTANTINOPLE | Pablo 2310833 |
| YOU GOT IT | Pablo 2310833 |
| ST. JAMES INFIRMARY | Pablo 2310833 |
| FOLLOW THE LEADER | Pablo 2310833 |
| OW | Pablo 2310833 |

**DIZZY GILLESPIE JAM**

Dizzy Gillespie, John Faddis (tp); Milt Jackson (vbs); Monty Alexander (p); Ray Brown (b); Jimmie Smith (d). *Switzerland. July 14, 1977.*

| | |
|---|---|
| GIRL OF MY DREAMS | Pablo 2308211 |
| GET HAPPY | Pablo 2308211 |
| ONCE IN A WHILE – BUT BEAUTIFUL – HERE'S THAT RAINY DAY (Medley) | Pablo 2308211 |
| THE CHAMP | Pablo 2308211 |
| HERE 'TIS | Pablo 2320105 |

Note: the above recordings took place at the Montreux Jazz Festival.

# DIZZY GILLESPIE

## A SELECTIVE DISCOGRAPHY

**DIZZY GILLESPIE**

Dizzy Gillespie (tp, jews harp); Toots Thielemans (g); Bernard Purdie (d). *Switzerland. July 19, 1980.*

| | |
|---|---|
| CHRISTOPHER COLUMBUS | Pablo Live D2308226 |
| I'M SITTING ON TOP OF THE WORLD | Pablo Live D2308226 |
| MANTECA | Pablo Live D2308226 |
| GET THAT BOOTY | Pablo Live D2308226 |
| KISSES | Pablo Live D2308226 |

Note: the above recordings took place at the Montreux Jazz Festival.

**MONGO SANTAMARIA**

Mongo Santamaria (congos, bongos); Dizzy Gillespie (tp); Tommy Villariny (tp, cowbell); Allen Hoist (as, fl, bars, cello); Doug Harris (ts, fl); Toots Thielemans (harmonica); Milt Hamilton (p); Lee Smith (b); Steve Berrios (d, timbales). *Switzerland. July 19, 1980.*

| | |
|---|---|
| VIRTUE | Pablo Live D2308229 |
| AFRO BLUE | Pablo Live D2308229 |
| SUMMERTIME | Pablo Live D2308229 |
| MAMBO MONGO | Pablo Live D2308229 |

Note: the above recordings took place at the Montreux Jazz Festival.

# DIZZY GILLESPIE

## A SELECTIVE DISCOGRAPHY

**DIZZY GILLESPIE**

Dizzy Gillespie (tp); James Moody (reeds); Ed Cherry (g); Mike Howell (b); George Hughes (d). *Switzerland. July 17, 1981.*

| | |
|---|---|
| MANTECA | Pablo Live D2620116 |
| CON ALMA | Pablo Live D2620116 |
| S.J.K. | Pablo Live D2620116 |
| NIGHT IN TUNISIA | Pablo Live D2620116 |
| BROTHER KING | Pablo Live D2620116 |
| BODY AND SOUL | Pablo Live D2620116 |
| TANGA | Pablo Live D2620116 |
| OLINGA | Pablo Live D2620116 |

**DIZZY GILLESPIE AND ARTURO SANDOVAL**

Dizzy Gillespie, Arturo Sandoval (tp); Esko Linnavalli (p); Pekka Sarmanto (b); Esko Rosnell (d). *Helsinki, Finland. September 9, 1982.*

| | |
|---|---|
| WHEATLEIGH HALL | Pablo 2310889 |
| FIRST CHANCE | Pablo 2310889 |
| AND THEN SHE STOPPED | Pablo 2310889 |
| RIMSKY | Pablo 2310889 |
| DIZZY THE DUCK | Pablo 2310889 |

Note: percussion effects can be heard on some of the above tracks.

# DIZZY GILLESPIE

## Titles of LP's

in the main discography, country of issue and further issue details.

| | |
|---|---|
| PM42408 | Dizzy Gillespie Vol 1/2 (1946-1948) – France. |
| LP4 | Dizzy's Delight – U.S.A. |
| LP2 | The small groups (1945-1946) – U.S.A. |
| BDL2006 | 20 golden pieces of Dizzy Gillespie. |
| PR24030 | In the beginning – United Kingdom/U.S.A. |
| Nost7629 | Dizzy Gillespie at the Downbeat Club, summer 1947 – Sweden. |
| DRLP34 | Bebop enters Sweden 1947-1949 – Sweden. |
| JR141 | Dizzy Gillespie Vol 3. |
| SJL2209 | Dee Gee days – U.S.A. |
| SJL2254 | Cool California – U.S.A. |
| JR137 | Dizzy Gillespie Vol 2. |
| 2610045 | Diz and Getz – France. 2 LP. Verve (J) MV2517. |
| MV2671 | Diz big band – Japan. |
| 96-0300-1 | One night in Washington – International. |
| MV2590 | World statesman – Japan. |
| MV2630 | Dizzy in Greece – Japan. |
| 46-146 | Live in hi-fi from Birdland summer 1956 – U.S.A. |
| 2304348 | Dizzy Gillespie at Newport – West Germany. |
| MV2620 | Dizzy Gillespie with Mary Lou Williams at Newport – Japan. |
| 2304382 | The greatest trumpet of them all. |
| MV2605 | An electrifying evening – Japan. |
| MV2696 | Have trumpet will excite – Japan. |
| 6336303 | Something old something new – Europe. |

# DIZZY GILLESPIE

Titles of LP's

| | |
|---|---|
| 6337203 | Dizzy Gillespie and The Double Six of Paris. Phillips (Am) EXPR 1034. |
| JAS5 | Swing low, sweet Cadillac – United Kingdom. MCA29036 (Am). |
| MPS15207 | Reunion big band. |
| Festival 215 | The great modern jazz trumpet, Dizzy Gillespie – France. |
| MRL5004 | In concert. |
| 30AM6133 | The Giant – France. Jazz Man (Am) 5017. |
| 30AM6135 | The source – France. Jazz Man (Am) 5021. |

Pablo issue numbers are the same in (Eu) and (Am) so no country of issue is noted.

| | |
|---|---|
| 2310719 | Dizzy Gillespie's big four. |
| 2310740 | Oscar Peterson and Dizzy Gillespie. |
| 2310771 | Afro Cuban moods. |
| 2310749 | Dizzie at the Montreux Festival 1975. |
| 2625708 | Bahiana – 2 LP. |
| 2625707 | Highlights of the Montreux Jazz Festival 1975 – 2 LP. |
| 2310781 | Carter Gillespie Inc. |
| 2310784 | Dizzy's party. |
| 2310794 | Free ride. |
| 2310833 | The gifted ones. |
| 2308211 | Jam Montreux '77. |
| 2308226 | Dizzy Gillespie Digital at Montreux 1980. |
| 2308229 | Mongo Santamaria with Dizzy Gillespie and Toots Thielmans. Digital at Montreux 1980. |
| 2620116 | Dizzy Gillespie – Musician – Composer – Raconteur – 2 LP. |
| 2310889 | To a Finland Station. |

# DIZZY GILLESPIE

Further listening suggestions:

Dizzy Gillespie rarities 1944/1961 – Raretone 5015 – FC – Italy. Good cross selection including early sides with Sarah Vaughan, a film sound track, concert and t.v. recordings.

Afro Cuban Bop – Circala BLJ8028 – Italy. October 1948 radio broadcasts by the big band.

The birth of modern jazz – Music for Pleasure 2MO56-64847 – France. Selections from 1944-1946 including some titles with Charlie Parker. Note: other Parker/Gillespie recording are listed in Brian Priestley's book *Charlie Parker* (Spellmount Hippocrene).

Dizzy Gillespie composed and arranged GRAND CENTRAL GETAWAY for the Jimmy Dorsey Orchestra. This title recorded for V-Discs July 20, 1944 has been issued on Hindsight HSR153 – U.S.A.

The title SWEET LORRAINE by the King Cole Trio mentioned in the text is on MCA MCL1671 – United Kingdom.

Dizzy Gillespie 1948-1952 – Queen Disc Q045 – Italy. Two titles from 1948 featuring Chano Pozo, balance are 1952 broadcasts from "Birdland".
Dizzy Gillespie and Sonny Stitt, 1975, all star date – Sonet (Eu) SNTF692.
Dizzy Gillespie and Benny Carter, 1954 session – Verve (J) MV2549.

Selections from the 1980 Aurex Jazz Festival. Japan – East World (J) EWJ80189.
Composer's concepts (1962-64) – Mercury (Am) EMS2-410. 2 LP.
Trumpet summit (with Clarke Terry, Freddie Hubbard) – Pablo 2312114.
The trumpet kings – Pablo 2310754.
Oscar Peterson Jam – Pablo 2308208.
The trumpet kings and Joe Turner – Pablo 2310717.

Further listening suggestions:

Dizzy Gillespie with Roy Eldridge, Oscar Peterson Trio – Pablo 2310816.
The best of Dizzy Gillespie – Pablo 2310855.

Norman Granz Jam Sessions and "Jazz at the Philharmonic" concerts issued on Verve.
Teddy Hill – RCA1937.
Cab Calloway – Columbia/CBS – 1939/1941.
Lionel Hampton – RCA Set 39.
Pete Brown – Decca 1942.
Lucky Millinder – Decca 1942.

Coleman Hawkins 1944; Billy Eckstine 1944; Oscar Pettiford 1945; Joe Marsala 1945; Clyde Hart 1945; Tony Scott 1945; Boyd Raeburn 1945; George Auld 1945 (one title on Phoenix LP4).

# Bibliography

Leonard Feather, *Inside Be-bop*, New York.

Alun Morgan and Raymond Horricks, *Modern Jazz, A Survey Of Developments Since 1939*, Victor Gollancz, London.

Ed. by Nat Hentoff and Nat Shapiro, *Hear Me Talkin' To Ya*,Rinehart, New York, Cassell, London.

Ed. by Nat Hentoff and Nat Shapiro, *The Jazz Makers*, Rinehart, New York. Not published in GB.

Ross Russell, *Bird Lives!* New York, Quartet Books, London.

*Dizzy Gillespie, An Autobiography*, New York, London.

*Inside Be-bop, Modern Jazz* and *Bird Lives!* all contain details of Dizzy's involvement with Charlie Parker in the early period of modern jazz. *Hear Me Talkin' To Ya*, has many statements by other musicians about the same events. In his chapter *The Jazz Makers* Leonard Feather returns to the subject and writes a full-length profile of Gillespie as both man and musician. The best-known magazine article is still Richard Boyer's in *The New Yorker*.